MUNDANEUM

Mel Croucher

MUNDANEUM

the shocking true story of the man who created the Internet and the man who destroyed it

Mel Croucher

Mundaneum: The Shocking True Story of the Man who Created the Internet and the Man who Destroyed It by Mel Croucher

First edition published in Great Britain in 2024 by Extremis Publishing Ltd., Suite 218, Castle House, 1 Baker Street, Stirling, FK8 1AL, United Kingdom.
www.extremispublishing.com

Extremis Publishing is a Private Limited Company registered in Scotland (SC509983) whose Registered Office is Suite 218, Castle House, 1 Baker Street, Stirling, FK8 1AL, United Kingdom.

Copyright © Mel Croucher, 2024.

Mel Croucher has asserted the moral right under the Copyright, Designs and Patents Act 1988 to be identified as the author of this work.

The views expressed in this work are solely those of the author, and do not necessarily reflect those of the publisher. The publisher hereby disclaims any responsibility for them.

This book is a work of non-fiction. Unless otherwise noted, the authors and the publisher make no explicit guarantees as to the accuracy of the information included in this book and, in some cases, the names of people, places and organisations may have been altered to protect their privacy. All hyperlinks were believed to be live and correctly detailed at the time of publication.

This book may include references to organisations, feature films, television programmes, popular songs, musical bands, novels, reference books, and other creative works, the titles of which are trademarks and/or registered trademarks, and which are the intellectual properties of their respective copyright holders.

All rights reserved. No part of this publication may be reproduced, stored in a retrieval system, or transmitted, in any form or by any means, electronic, mechanical, photocopying, recording or otherwise, without the prior permission in writing of the publisher.

This book is sold subject to the condition that it shall not, by way of trade or otherwise, be lent, re-sold or hired out, or otherwise circulated without the publisher's prior consent in any form of binding or cover other than that in which it is published and without a similar condition including this condition being imposed on the subsequent purchaser.

A CIP catalogue record for this book is available from the British Library.

ISBN: 978-1-7394845-6-9

Typeset in Merriweather.

Printed and bound in Great Britain by IngramSpark, Chapter House, Pitfield, Kiln Farm, Milton Keynes, MK11 3LW, United Kingdom.

Cover artwork is Copyright © Mel Croucher, all rights reserved.
Cover design and book design is Copyright © Mel Croucher.
Author images are Copyright © Mel Croucher, all rights reserved.

Internal photographic images are sourced from the author's private collections unless otherwise stated in the Photographic and Pictorial Images section, which forms an extension to this legal page.

The copyrights of third parties are reserved. All third party imagery is used under the provision of Fair Use for the purposes of commentary and criticism. While every reasonable effort has been made to contact copyright holders and secure permission for all images reproduced in this work, we offer apologies for any instances in which this was not possible and for any inadvertent omissions.

MUNDANEUM

This is the true story of two men who meet only once for half an hour.

One is a Belgian pacifist named Paul Otlet, and the other is a German Nazi named Hans Hagemeyer.

Both men are visionaries, but their visions for the future of the world cannot be more different.

Paul Otlet's vision is to promote peace through global access to information, and he builds a world-wide-web to deliver exactly that.

Hans Hagemeyer's vision is to harness information to control the masses, and for a while he achieves that too.

All of the characters in this book exist historically, and they are portrayed as accurately as possible using original source material.

All of the events happen in the locations depicted and on the dates given.

Quoted extracts from published documents are translated into English from the original, and colloquialised by the author.

Conversational text is created by the author to reflect the thoughts, opinions and declarations of the speakers, gathered from original writings by them and about them.

ABOUT THE AUTHOR

Mel Croucher is the acknowledged founder of the British computer games industry. Originally an architect, he moved into gaming "to force my weird music on an unwilling public."

Among his innovations, he pioneered the first radio broadcasts of computer software, the first interactive soap opera, the first real-world adventure quest, the first computer-generated movie, the first AI virtual companion and the first million-user viral marketing campaign.

He is the author of text books, technical manuals, fiction and non-fiction, and over a thousand of his columns, investigations and cartoon strips have appeared in print over five decades.

A BRIEF HISTORY

9 March 1999
US Vice-President Al Gore declares on CNN, "During my service in the United States Congress, I took the initiative in creating the Internet."

12 March 1989
Tim Berners-Lee proposes a shared information system using hypertext. He is knighted "for inventing the world wide web."

1 January 1983
The US Defense Data Network officially adopts Transmission Control Protocol, recognised by many as the birth of the Internet.

21 August 1962
Joseph Licklider describes a global network for interconnected computers to access data from remote sites.

4 July 1961
Leonard Kleinrock publishes a proposal for an online network of machines to communicate through packets of information.

23 April 1910
Long, long ago, before any of the above, Paul Otlet opens his world wide web to the public. He names it the Mundaneum.

PART ONE

PAUL OTLET

THE MAN WHO INVENTED
THE INTERNET

Chapter 1

23 August 1876
67 Rue Neuve, Brussels, Belgium

The Egomaniac sweeps into Studio Dupont. He is rich. His beard is royal. He has vision. He has just built a railway line from the capital to the coast. His communication network is spreading throughout the cities of Europe. Through Florence, through Prague, through Dusseldorf and through Odessa. He intends to change the face of the world with his timetabled travel. One by one his tramways rattle and hum, dragged by horses, owned by bankers, used by anyone who can afford a few centimes to take a ride across the city.

In the studio reception room, the Egomaniac shoves his son towards Madame Dupont, as he waves away the family business card she proffers on a small silver tray. The card is heavily embossed. The print is in Italics.

Studio Dupont, established 1864.
Photographers to the diplomatic corps, the great bodies of state, the magistrature, the army, the ministries, the public administration, the world of letters, science and the arts. Publisher of the Belgian Panthéon.

The Egomaniac snarls that he already has her card, and in any case he ticks all the boxes for each of those categories. He is the great Edouard Otlet. Today his elder son Paul is to have his photographic portrait taken by the renowned Monsieur Henri Dupont.

A dapper man steps into the room. He remembers this child. He is a photographer. He has a photographic memory. He first captures the boy's image several years ago, posed cradled in his mother's arms as she looks down at her baby in fond profile. The photographer remembers that session well for a reason. It is also the day of his first commission to capture the image of royalty. His other subject on that day is Princess Josephine Caroline in a half-length portrait, her plump little face to camera. She is three years old, squirming like a pink eel. But Dupont remembers that the subject in front of him now is as distinctively different now as he was back then. Unlike most other infants, this little creature is remarkably sentient, very still, staring intently at the index files of client accounts and photographic plates. Focussed and unblinking.

The Egomaniac goes outside for a smoke, and to admire the rails of his own tramline that gleam along the bank of the *Canal de Bruxelles* opposite the studio front door. The bells of Sainte Catherine clang the hour nearby. He checks his pocket watch, knowing a tram is due. Sure enough, in less than a minute an ornate yellow vehicle appears, drawn by two brown horses. Only half a dozen men ride the open top deck, sitting along the bench that runs its length, their feet up on the kickboards. One of them throws a marijuana cigarette stub into the canal. Apart from the conductor and the driver the lower deck is empty. The Egomaniac frowns and puzzles as to why business is so bad.

In the studio, the boy is left standing in front of a camera tripod. He is dressed in a juvenile military jacket with a floppy silk bow tied loose below a starched white collar. His hair is a soft blond. The end of his nose tilts upwards. The photographer attempts to make small-talk in an effort to relax his young subject.

"It's Paul, isn't it? Yes, Paul. So tell me Paul, have you been anywhere nice for your summer holidays?"

"No Sir. I had to go Westende, to Father's hunting estate again. It is very boring there. I like it better when we have to go to Moscow."

"You have been to Moscow?"

"Yes Sir. They speak French there, but it sounds funny."

"Splendid! So, Paul my boy, how is your mother?"

"My mother is dead, Sir. She has been dead these five years."

"Aah, yes, I see. Yes, I see. I was, I am, so sad to hear that. But how are you getting on at school, Paul? Do you have many friends there?"

"I do not go to school, Sir. I take my lessons at home. I do not have any friends. I have a younger brother. His name is Maurice. My brother Maurice also takes his lessons at home."

"Ah, yes. How very nice for you."

"It is not really very nice for me, Sir."

"Hmm. Yes, I mean, no. Ah, now Paul, we are going to make a very special photograph today, and I will need you to remain quite still while I count to one hundred and let this camera capture your image without it becoming all fuzzy. Please can you try very hard not to blink. Can you do that for me?"

The boy nods. His eyes remain unblinking.

"So Paul, do you have any questions before I begin the exposure of your photographic plate?"

Paul Otlet knows how cameras work. He understands the photographic process and the need for a static subject. He stares at the rows of filing cabinets, each with an identification card in a polished brass holder on the front of the sliding wooden box drawers.

"Yes, Sir, yes I have a question. Um, I think that you make several photographs each day, and well, that will be a great many photographs. And for each photograph you will keep a record. My question is, how do you keep your records in order? I mean, is it by date, or is it by a name, or is it by what a person pays you? I know you made my photograph here before, so ... how do you do it?"

"Oh. Well. Goodness me. Yes. Well, it is by alphabetical order of the name of my clients, and also by the subject in the picture? But why do you ask such a thing ... what interests you?"

"Well, Sir, what interests me is, before you sent Madame Dupont to greet my father just now, how long did it take you to find his record?"

The photographer tries to fathom the boy's expressionless stare. He is nonplussed.

"How old are you, Paul?"

"Today is my eighth birthday, Sir. That is why I am here. You are to make my birthday portrait and add it to the record. Then you will index and file it so it can be put away in my father's account and retrieved for next time."

Inauguration Day of the Brussels tramway, 1874

Paul Otlet and his mother, 1868

Paul on his 8th birthday

Chapter 2

September 1881
Lycée Louis-le-Grand, Paris, France

Paul is soon to leave childhood behind. He is introspective and obsessive and he keeps an introspective diary obsessively. The diary reveals that his pre-teen years are friendless and oppressed by the whims of his father, but this oppression leads to precocious activity. For his own amusement, he pressgangs his younger brother Maurice to help him draw up an elaborate framework for an index of ideas that he calls *The Limited Company of Useful Knowledge*. It is a foreshadowing of what becomes Paul Otlet's lifetime obsession.

Educated at home in Brussels, Paul has a very contradictory childhood. Sometimes he is spirited away on far-flung holidays at the command of his father, but most of the time he is confined to the friendless isolation of the family home with only books for company. Then, with a shocking suddenness, this shy and nervous youngster is wrenched from his family home and transplanted to the Latin Quarter of Paris, to a vast dilapidated boarding school full of boys exiled and kennelled from all corners of Europe. The school is run by Jesuits. His father's business is going through a rocky patch and the Egomaniac is currently away in Moscow trying to raise more funds. Before he leaves, he packs his son off to be shaped, honed and moulded by these fierce Catholics. As well as his other woes, the boy now has the disciplines of Jesus to contend with.

In a few years time, with his railway and tram empire back on track, the boy's father runs the election campaign for the Catholic Party in the province of Luxembourg, and finds himself elected to the Senate under new proportional representation rules. The Catholics sweep to power with a hefty majority over the combined opposition of socialists and liberals. If Jesus saves, then the least Edouard Otlet can do in anticipation of the inevitable salvation is to commit his elder son to the priests for a modest fee.

The most Paul can do in anticipation of the inevitable salvation is to seek sanctuary, and his habitual sanctuary is sought in books. Paul Otlet is now thirteen years old, so he is of an age where he is allowed to abandon the school smock in favour of a brass buttoned jacket and trousers with a military side-stripe, and today is a typical day when he visits the lycée library as soon as lessons end.

The library is vast, it is over three hundred years old. One day in 1918 it gets hit by a German shell fired by a weapon of mass destruction called Big Bertha. Fifty years after that it becomes the venue that triggers the international student revolution of '68. But today it is where Paul Otlet's singular life is hit by a personal bombshell and revolutionised. It is the day that he picks up a five-year-old issue of *The Library Journal*, published by the American Department of Education. His attention is drawn to it because the journal lies under the beam of an electric desk lamp, an invention he has never encountered before.

Paris is already known as the city of light, and the recent innovation of harsh electrically-powered street lamps illuminates the night. Recently there is talk of placing huge electric searchlights to pierce the heavens from the top of a gigantic iron tower planned by Monsieur Eiffel, but planning permission is not certain for another three years. On the other hand, this little indoor device is something of the here and now. It has a stubby goose-neck stand, and a shade with an integral focussing glass to create a very subtle circle of light. Behind the glass, a glowing onion bulb feels warm when Paul extends a hand towards it.

Paul's privately tutored English is not up to the job of absorbing the item in the American *Journal*, but someone has left the book open with a sheet of notes written in French that not only speaks to him, but sings. The notes are by the Lycée's librarian, Anatole Bailly who is a civilian as opposed to a Jesuit. Bailly is in his late fifties, clean shaven and considered by some to be extremely good looking. He comes from a moderately wealthy family and his father is director of a large auditing company, which is why Bailly has made notes to accompany a copy of the American item. He intends to send it to his aged father because he thinks it will tickle his fancy. In fact, the librarian's real passion is not for numbers at all, but for Greek, and his *Dictionaire Grec-Français* becomes very famous indeed before the end of the century.

The boy's face flushes, and he hangs his head.

"Please Sir, I apologise for moving this volume, but it was left open by the reading lamp."

"Ah, Otlet. You haunt our shelves again. And why did you move it?"

"I was trying to understand the English words, Sir."

"So, are you interested in numbers, my boy?"

"Yes Sir, but I am more interested in the mathematics of language."

The librarian thinks this is a remarkable thing for such a young person to say. In fact he thinks it is a remarkable thing for someone of any age to say, but it chimes with his own beliefs concerning the universality of language. He sits the boy down, adjusts the reading lamp and carefully begins to translate the item, pausing every now and then as Paul absorbs and acknowledges each point.

The item is by a New York librarian called Melvil Dewey who in 1876 invents a classification system for indexing, shelving and retrieving books. It's all based on simple numbers. Still in his twenties, Melvil Dewey is granted copyright on the first edition of his index, which consists of two thousand categories held on little cards and stored in box-files. This is rather like the filing system in Dupont's photographic studio back in Brussels, only much, much better.

Soon Dewey's copyright grows to cover over ten thousand precisely defined categories. Not only can it index any ancient volume in an ancient library like this one, but it can index all future volumes in all future libraries. For example, in ninety-three years time, the code for the Internet is added to Dewey's original system with the listing *Information > Computation > Network > = 004.678*.

Paul spends a lot of time in the library. He can be found here most days, and he is not the first person to dream of a universal goldmine of all the world's knowledge, but he is probably the first to see it as a way to change the future. Not yet, but soon.

He learns about the libraries of ancient Sumeria, where the reference codes are written in a gridded matrix of little straight lines. He reads of the Great Library of Alexandria in Egypt, accidentally burned to ashes by a man calling himself Julius Caesar. He is intrigued by how the Vatican Library tries to gather all human knowledge over the centuries and then the Pope tries to ban access to it, much as the Emperor Shi Huangdi tries to do long before there was a man calling himself Julius Caesar.

But there is another man who intrigues Paul Otlet far more than any pope or emperor, and his name is Conrad Gessner, born in Zurich in 1516. As well as being a physician and a naturalist, Gessner is also a librarian with a big ambition. He labours to create a *Universal Bibliography* of all the world's published knowledge, and he develops an indexing technique to catalogue every plant and every animal in the known world, writing them down on individual slips of paper and organising them in a way that is completely logical to Paul. Then Gessner experiences a revelation, when he figures out that this same technique can be used not only for living things but for everything and anything at all.

Gessner creates the same sort of library index cards that this Dewey from America has managed to get a patent on two centuries later. Meanwhile in the German university of Leipzig, the famed Gottfried Leibniz, philosopher and inventor of calculus, waits until Gessner is dead and forgotten and steals his idea of a user-based filing system. Only he takes it a step further and builds an intricate cabinet to house it in.

And then another breakthrough comes, and it is not caused by the sacred but by the profane. It is the repurposing of the humble playing card. Playing cards are universal throughout Europe. When at home, Paul plays *Solitaire* with packs of his father's cards, and he often lays them out to form a patterns and sequences. Playing cards are more or less a standard size, they are durable and the reverse side of the cheapest packs are blank. And they are often used for other purposes. For example they can be popped into a drawer, flipped, shuffled, re-ordered and used as a random-access card index, which is not much use to most of humanity but which is of great use to librarians. Most libraries are too small to warrant such a thing, but this vast library in which Paul Otlet finds himself is absolutely perfect.

He spends his remaining time at Lycée Louis-le-Grand applying the Dewey system here. The Jesuit brothers don't exactly endorse his pursuit, but it's better than many of the disgusting activities the other thirteen year-olds indulge in. And as the librarian Anatole Bailly monitors Paul's progress, the great man glows with satisfaction, as warm and bright as his personal electric reading lamp. This boy has a very bright future ahead of him, as long as the Jesuits do not meddle with his brain too much.

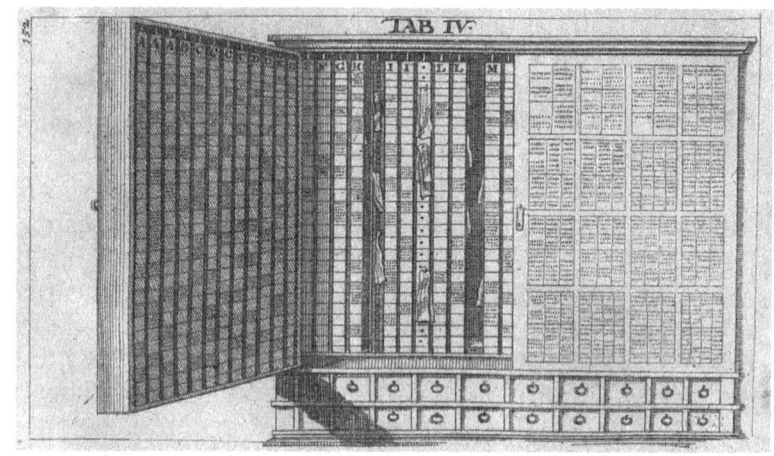

the Leibniz random access database, 1689

Lycée Louis-le-Grand, 1881

Anatole Bailly, librarian, 1881

DIVISIONS.

0			**500**	**Natural Science.**
10	Bibliography.		510	Mathematics.
20	Book Rarities.		520	Astronomy.
30	General Cyclopedias.		530	Physics.
40	Polygraphy.		540	Chemistry.
50	General Periodicals.		550	Geology.
60	General Societies.		560	Paleontology.
70			570	Biology.
80			580	Botany.
90			590	Zoology.
100	**Philosophy.**		**600**	**Useful Arts.**
110	Metaphysics.		610	Medicine.
120			620	Engineering.
130	Anthropology.		630	Agriculture.
140	Schools of Psychology.		640	Domestic Economy.
150	Mental Faculties.		650	Communication and Commerce.
160	Logic.		660	Chemical Technology.
170	Ethics.		670	Manufactures.
180	Ancient Philosophies.		680	Mechanic Trades.
190	Modern Philosophies.		690	Building.
200	**Theology.**		**700**	**Fine Arts.**
210	Natural Theology.		710	Landscape Gardening.
220	Bible.		720	Architecture.
230	Doctrinal Theology.		730	Sculpture.
240	Practical and Devotional.		740	Drawing and Design.
250	Homiletical and Pastoral.		750	Painting.
260	Institutions and Missions.		760	Engraving.
270	Ecclesiastical History.		770	Photography.
280	Christian Sects.		780	Music.
290	Non-christian Religions.		790	Amusements.
300	**Sociology.**		**800**	**Literature.**
310	Statistics.		810	Treatises and Collections.
320	Political Science.		820	English.
330	Political Economy.		830	German.
340	Law.		840	French.
350	Administration.		850	Italian.
360	Associations and Institutions.		860	Spanish.
370	Education.		870	Latin.
380	Commerce and Communication.		880	Greek.
390	Customs and Costumes.		890	Other Languages.
400	**Philology.**		**900**	**History.**
410	Comparative.		910	Geography and Description.
420	English.		920	Biography.
430	German.		930	Ancient History.
440	French.		940	Europe.
450	Italian.		950	Asia.
460	Spanish.		960	Africa.
470	Latin.		970	North America.
480	Greek.		980	South America.
490	Other Languages.		990	Oceanica and Polar Regions.

(940–990 bracketed as Modern.)

Melvil Dewey decimal categories, 1876

Chapter 3

July 1891
Brussels, Belgium

Paul is a widely-travelled young man, extracted from education whenever his father feels like dragging him far and wide. He experiences several corners of France, Italy and Russia while still in his teens, and records the events in his diaries. When business booms, the Egomaniac buys a chunk of a Mediterranean island called Île du Levant. A century later it becomes a nudist colony. Back in Paul's time, there are lessons in music and dance, there is hunting, fishing and shooting, there is *Nora* the family yacht, and by all appearances everything should be idyllic. But Paul's diaries reveal the melancholy and guilt of a self-obsessed young man with time on his hands and the luxury of wealth, recently moulded by those Jesuits in Paris.

"My life is more and more closed in on itself. I cannot tolerate the vanity of the world. I desire to lead a life given over to the abstractions of science. On the other hand there is a great emptiness in my heart which I must also fill. God alone is capable of filling this emptiness and it is what I ask of Him. To improve my life, this is what I want to live for and I must battle against myself and my innate weakness."

Over time, Paul matures and grows out of these thoughts and he becomes increasingly involved in the sciences. He builds a natural history collection as a hobby, while convincing himself that he needs to follow some sort of pathway that contributes to the wellbeing of society and fulfil his duty as a citizen. And then, declaring that he has studied both Christianity and science in great detail, he suddenly turns his back on both and announces that he will become a lawyer.

After graduating from the Free University a year ago, Paul is in possession of a law degree, but he finds arguing the legal toss most unsatisfying. He is much more interested in hard facts, and embraces his true love of bibliography. He also embraces his cousin Fernande Gloner, marries her, and she delivers two sons, Marcel and Jean, in double-quick time.

In the beginning, Paul revels in his love and his marriage to this woman who seems so demure, meek and mild. But she soon reveals herself as an airhead. She is childish, wilful, and not in the slightest bit interested in his work. She runs up huge bills at the dressmakers, and overspends by taking the boys on numerous visits to see her extended family of affluent bankers in Berlin. In his diary Paul quotes her own words when she says, "Darling, .I will always be a little nothing, but you must love me just as I am. I am a naughty little girl, I know, and I make you cry. But don't be lonely."

Almost as if acting on her instructions, Paul avoids loneliness by joining a slew of clubs and associations, including the exclusive Circle of Young Barristers in Brussels. He begins to publish a few articles in their house magazine *Palais*, but he remains as disillusioned as ever. Disillusioned, that is, until he meets an older man.

In between impregnating his new wife and dealing with the aftermath, Paul finds the time to form a partnership and friendship with a fellow-lawyer fourteen years his senior called Henri La Fontaine. Paul is an intern in the office of Edmond Picard, who is a renowned legal figure with a growing reputation as a writer too. It is Picard who introduces the two men whose future relationship is key to one half of this story, Paul Otlet and Henri La Fontaine. They are tasked with working together to produce a book of case law, which pays he rent but which is very boring. Much more interesting to both of them is the whole world of books, libraries and of bibliography.

La Fontaine not only shares Paul's passion for books but introduces him to the concept of harnessing the written word to promote international relations based on peace and mutual trade. This marks the beginning of a lifelong friendship between the two men which lasts for over fifty years, encompassing election to the Senate, winning the Nobel Peace Prize, growing impressive facial hair and the invention of the Internet.

Paul is a lifelong obsessive diarist, and now he starts to write pamphlets as well. He often indulges his wife's wishes to eat out in lavish restaurants in the company of his family and her friends, but on this fine summer evening, after dining at home with La Fontaine, Paul is reading aloud from a newly-published pamphlet he has written. His boys are too young to understand the meaning behind nursery rhymes, let alone their father's lecture. Their mother cocks her head to one side, and smiles the way a good Germanic Belgian wife in 1891 is expected to smile. On the other hand, Henri La Fontaine is absolutely astounded by the clarity of his new friend's ideas as he tries to keep up with Paul's train of thought.

Paul's publication is called *A Little Thing About Bibliography* and the flowing French goes like this, condensed into chunks from the carcass of the original and translated into English. He starts to read aloud at a slow pace.

"Are you sitting comfortably? Then I'll begin. Ahem. The debasement of all kinds of publication is alarming to those of us who are concerned about quality rather than quantity. What exactly is original in any of these books, brochures or journals? What allowances must be made for style and repetition? What is really new? This is a delicate but vital question. If one spends a bit of time reading new works, it seems that everything has already been said, that everything to be said is already known, and that further reading is pointless. This belief causes scepticism, the consequences of which are deplorable."

La Fontaine nods his head in agreement as Paul gets into his stride.

"Seeing that so much is based only on opinion, I am constrained to believe that facts are too complex to be captured by any kind of conceptual formula, because facts are always too exclusive and too tyrannical. It follows that social sciences are not seen as one discipline in terms of their conclusions, but as a bunch of personal opinions based on documents thrown together without any order or method.

Let's compare this against the great works of the natural sciences. The difference between them is that in the natural sciences, speculation and interpretation are secondary, and most of the time they are hardly ever made at all. The results of the natural sciences are based on millions of carefully observed facts, which are then analysed and catalogued. These facts have been integrated into sequences, and the combination of these sequences has led to the declaration of laws and rules, from which the most powerful and indestructible synthesis that has ever been made now seems possible."

Paul pauses, and looks at his little audience, unblinking. His wife sports her default expression of bemusement, which often gives way to one of wide-eyed vacancy. One of their children seems to be drooling for no apparent reason and the other watches on. His friend Henri gives him a modest fist-pump of encouragement, so Paul continues.

"Ingenious brains have always popped up to invent new research instruments needed to demonstrate the progress of science. But all of this equipment would be worth very little if all the natural scientists in the world had not worked toward the completion of the same task, the broad outline of whose design has been impressed upon each one of them.

Never has their activity been better co-ordinated. Never has there been less duplication. It seems they are always aware of the current state of their science, that they never have to work in vain covering the same old ground, and rediscovering without realising it what was already known. Moreover, each new discovery and each new contribution to the advancement of their science seems to be recorded immediately, and becomes the point of departure for future research.

The chemist's whole universe is contained in the test tubes of his laboratory. The physicist experiments with natural forces which are the same in Europe, India and Australia. The dogs, piglets and rabbits needed for vivisection are found in every latitude. But social facts? They constitute data of which both the whole and its parts escape the wisest observer."

Fernande erupts into a giggling fit at the mention of dogs, piglets and rabbits, probably with relief, as these are the first words that have sparked her interest. Henri pretends not to notice the interruption until the boys join in the fun as their mother makes little piglet noises in their faces, and then even Henri can't resist and he mimes imaginary rabbit whiskers. But the boys are getting drowsy now, and after this comic relief Paul carries on reading from his script.

"Judgments here are as complex as the matters judged. Any error in any one of them has immediate consequences for everything that's deduced from it, in other words it multiplies the error to infinity. So it's vital that the best minds need to look at the overall organisation of the work, and to bring together its best results. Individual monographs, detailed research and contributions to studies are multiplying out of all proportion, as are the facts and figures that go with them."

Paul looks up and points at Henri La Fontaine. He is about to reveal his proposal for the future.

"I propose that these individual works are registered and classified, so that anyone can retrieve them immediately in order to use them and push ahead, to know at any moment what has been done and what remains to be done.

Up until now, very little has been accomplished along these lines! What could be easier for an explorer than to know precisely and instantly the areas towards which they must direct their investigations if new territory is to be added to the known world. Is it not the same for industrial discoveries? Each country has a patent office which registers every new invention and publishes a daily journal to keep the industrial world abreast of progress. Would it be so difficult to achieve a similar registration of sociological data and concepts?

It is important to direct individual efforts towards a common goal and not to waste anyone's time and energy. Not that it should be necessary to recreate an ideas-factory along the lines of the vast factories created for the production of goods. There each person, without any regard for their tastes and skills, is given a specific task to do. He patiently works away at one of a thousand nuts and bolts which will be used for an infinitely complex machine that perhaps he never sees complete. Modern scientific research requires too much initiative for such procedures to be appropriate to it. Everyone's freedom must be maintained. But this principle is in no way incompatible with a common resource.

Is it possible to achieve this co-ordination, not by imposing rules of work on anyone, but by creating collective works which, while above and beyond individual projects, use them, complete them, make their development easier? This is my question in a nutshell.

The indexing of knowledge has been restricted to the modest function of listing their sources. In the beginning this was the preoccupation of the bibliophile, the librarian and the speculative book trade. Subsequently, with the publication of the catalogues of our great public libraries, it became more scientific. It was easy to arrange books alphabetically by the names of authors. A few large subject divisions were also created, but these were no more than literature, law, history, and so on. Gradually, for their own use, librarians constructed catalogues intended to respond to requests for information.

    The principle arrangement of such catalogues was classification by subject. It was necessary to know how to indicate immediately what books their library had on alcoholism, taxes, the history of the French Revolution, and on and on."

    Fernande picks up on the word alcoholism and enquires if anyone fancies a drink. This time, Henri clacks his tongue against the roof of his mouth, quietly but audibly, and the woman of the house remains seated. Paul does not acknowledge the interruption at all.

    "Then authors began to adopt the habit of referring whenever they could to the sources they had used. Scholars also imitated the example of librarians. They created their own small bibliographical listings where they recorded not only the resources of their own libraries but, culled from their reading, they recorded any bibliographical or other information which might be useful to them some day.

    They also began to refer to the collectors of detailed index cards, those who, because of their carefully arranged systems of drawers and pigeon-holes, could furnish material in a couple of hours for a scholarly lecture on any subject with which they were familiar. Anyone with research to do went and knocked on their door, certain of coming away with hands full of references. In this way, enormous trouble was avoided. Referral to the latest study to have appeared on a subject did away with the need for ploughing through mountains of books and journals as a means of being brought up to date on it. They came so far but they hardly went any further.

My first step towards this sort of collective work would be to systematically approach the classification of sources. Stuff that has already been written and thought provides the basic materials of the social sciences. It is excellent for doing that. It is, therefore, quite natural at the outset to make a systematic inventory of everything - both historical and contemporary, a catalogue of everything in books, brochures, and journals, arranged systematically. This work can begin at once. It can fall into two series. One series is a retrospective of all knowledge assembled to date, and the other series is all new published knowledge to be updated month by month."

Paul now pauses for effect, and once again extends his index finger towards Henri.

"The work of my colleague Henri La Fontaine is important. He has asked the members of our national institutions to collaborate in the preparation of standard size data cards. Each person who agreed to be associated with our work has been given cards of the same format. The title of the book or item, the name of the author, that of the publisher, the price, the year, the number of pages and a short summary were all added to the card. But it failed. It didn't work, because everyone interpreted the indexing in their own way.

So what I propose is that we need to keep the standard size card index, which does work, and reduce the data to four elements: the facts, the interpretation of facts, the statistics and the sources. The data can then be brought together and re-arranged to answer any question that anyone can pose. The various parts of any book, or article, or lecture can be easily reduced to these four elements, not along the lines of the special plan of any particular publication, but according to the index appropriate to each element.

This systematic recording of facts, statistical data and interpretations need only be undertaken by a few individuals who will create a kind of artificial brain by means of cards containing actual information, notes and references."

There is a silence in the room. The children are asleep, so Fernande Otlet mimes an exaggerated hand-clap gesture in order not to disturb them. She understands little or nothing of what her husband has been reading aloud, whereas Henri understands every word. His new friend and colleague is proposing nothing less than a universal repository of all human knowledge, not as a dreamer's fantasy but as a practical plan based on existing technology.

Fernande asks if anyone fancies that drink, in a whisper so as not to wake the children. Then the telephone rings and wakes the children anyway. It is Paul's father phoning all the way from Paris.

The world's first public international telephone line is up and running between Brussels and the French capitol, open for business at the cost of three francs for five minutes. Brussels is ahead of the world in telephone access, with the Bell Telephone Company founding its headquarters right here in the city and now employing three dozen people.

The latest advance in telephony is the introduction of a rotary dial, which Paul likes a lot. Accessing people by giving them a unique identification number is such a simple and effective method. He often considers extending this method to apply such a personal telephone number to other applications. For example, a unique personal code number allocated at birth could be linked to a postal address, or marriage records, or even a whole family tree. It could help track bank accounts, work records, even the right to vote.

As Paul waits for the telephone connection to be made he turns to Henri and says, "Imagine if we could link my imaginary artificial brain index to all the imaginary libraries in the world by all the world's imaginary telephones!"

La Fontaine suppresses a stifled cough, but the boys are now wide awake again, and Fernande is on the move to find the source of that drink. Henri tries to process Paul's new proposal for a world-wide index to function as a network of universal reference and research. Then a mechanical sound comes from the telephone earpiece, followed by a metallic but familiar voice. Paul pulls a face, bends his head towards the mouthpiece and says,"Hello, Father?"

rotary dial telephone, 1891

Henri La Fontaine, 1891

Paul Otlet, 1891

Paul Otlet, seated centre-right, family and friends dine out, 1890

Chapter 4

July 1897
Tervueren Colonial Palace, Brussels, Belgium

Paul's new home is almost complete. Number 13 Rue de Florence is a magnificent Art Nouveau town house designed by the top local architect Octave van Rysselberghe. The structure is built of impressive ash-grey stone. Under the eaves, a frieze of gold fronds and scallop shells are painted on a blue background to encircle the entire structure. Stained-glass windows of stylised waves and curlicues illuminate the interiors, and a grand wooden staircase sweeps up the centre of the building in a high-gloss declaration of arrogance and entitlement.

Paul's father already has business interests in South America and New Guinea, and now he organises a self-indulgent expedition to the Congo to amass a collection of artifacts which he intends to exhibit in a self-glorifying Museum of Africana. But his museum never materialises. His egomania is responsible for major setbacks in his business empire, and a mixture of single-mindedness and recklessness causes bankruptcy for a significant slice of his companies. As an economic downturn hits before the new century dawns, he begins to sell off what he can salvage, but for now his son steers well clear of any involvement. Part of the Egomaniac's considerable art collection is auctioned off, and several major works find there way here, to adorn the walls of Paul's new home.

Today Paul decides not to monitor the final touches to the interior, but instead to take his sons to see how the other half lives, and conduct them on a family visit just outside of the city to the new Congo zoo. Paul has a free public transport season ticket, but he has to pay for his boys to ride the brand new tramline built by their grandfather on credit. His signature on the season ticket is scrawled and child-like. Father and sons ride together all the way to the pleasure gardens constructed by order of the King as a sort of palace of colonial celebration. Like Paul's new mansion, the zoo pavilions are presented in the latest Art Nouveau style, and as well as vast displays of exotic objects there is a hippodrome, a cycle track and a gymnastic arena.

It is supposed to be summer, but the weather is rubbish, continually cold and wet. Of the 267 live zoo specimens captured in the heat of the Congo and exhibited here in Brussels, seven of the tropical creatures fall ill and die in their enclosures. They not only succumb to the damp climate, but their forced diet is also completely wrong. The names of the males and females are recorded as Mpemba, Ngemba, Ekia, Nzau, Kitukwa and Mibange, and the name of the baby is Sambo.

Like all the other exhibits, they are of the human species but regarded as sub-human by most of the voyeurs. As soon as they die, the zookeepers bury their bodies in unconsecrated ground that is reserved for suicides and murderers. In 1953 their remains are disinterred and moved to the nearby courtyard of Saint John the Evangelist.

As for now, three fenced 'native villages' are sited near an artificial pond. Two are for Bangala people and one is for Mayombes, forced from their natural habitats and put on display to be stared at and pointed at. Although they have access to water, their feeding times are highly unpredictable, but their exhibitions of exotic dancing are regular as clockwork. There are also ninety soldiers from the so-called native *Force Publique* who are ordered to parade up and down for the entertainment of the crowds, on the hour, every hour.

There is a fourth enclosure, named Gijzegem, which is managed by a Flemish Abbot called Van Impe, who sets about the process of civilising these Congolese savages. He does this by teaching them to sing hymns, much to the amusement of the public. By the time the zoo closes in late

November, one million paying visitors pass through the turnstiles. On the day that Paul and the boys visit, *Le National* newspaper publishes an unusually discordant item that runs against the attitude of the majority. It reads like this.

Here they are, our black brothers, closely guarded by their own kin – our valiant African troops, our overzealous soldiers of the annexation of the Congo. They are there, benefiting from a marvellous décor, giving the impression of their life in the middle of it, set up like a fairground show, a fantasy Congo with pseudo-villages created as a counterpart to this zoo of branded black advertising. This is something quite degrading for humanity, to see these unfortunate people enclosed like animals, left to the distressing and degrading reflections of the white people who rush and pay to gawp at them on show.

Paul, is not much interested in the editorial views of the newspaper. His embracing of human rights is not yet on the agenda. He is more interested in the exhibition site itself. In collaboration with his friend Henri La Fontaine, he is working on a major proposal for presentation to the city authorities. His theories of a great repository of automated knowledge are coming along nicely, he needs a prestigious location in which to house it, and these new exhibition buildings seem to him to be the perfect venue. What he also needs now is a memorable brand-name for the project, a name that conveys something global and trustworthy. Something like Mondo Universalis, or Mundi Sciencia. Maybe Sapientium or Pan-Kosmia. Or perhaps World-Wide-Librarium? Paul knows that he needs to work on his branding before he can present anything to potential backers.

Paul Otlet's season ticket between Brussels & Tervueren

Colonial Palace 1897 Exhibition grounds

souvenir postcard of Colonial Palace human zoo exhibits, 1897

the Otlet Mansion, 1897

Chapter 5

September 1895
Staircase of the Jews, Hotel Ravenstein, Brussels

Paul is cock-a-hoop. He wins a commission from Belgium's prestigious Society of Social and Political Sciences, in recognition of his radical theories about libraries and revolutionary methods to catalogue and retrieve information. To tell the truth, it is Henri La Fontaine who is the main attraction for the Society, but professionally the two friends share everything that comes their way. Henri already has a very high profile for his political and social work. He is the founder of the Belgian League of Women's Rights, a member of the Labour Party since it was created, and most important of all he is recently elected to the Senate.

Now he hands Paul the commission to create bibliographies for the library system of the social sciences, and it takes the two men all of three years to put Paul's theories into practice.

Never one for false modesty, Paul names their enterprise *The International Federation for Information and Documentation* even though it is not international and even though the La Fontaine and Otlet federation consists of nothing but a handshake. And also, never one to be restricted by ambition, Paul extends their remit to cover not just the social sciences but every subject known to humanity. To make it all work he needs to contact the man who has been his hero since he was a schoolboy, the American inventor of the Dewey Decimal classification system for libraries, Melvil Dewey himself.

Paul unashamedly embellishes the reputation of his famous partner, and writes Dewey a wheedling letter asking permission to modify and expand the index system to cover any publication, any fact, or any item of knowledge, and put them into a centralised data resource. Dewey is flattered but suspicious of this young Belgian and his socialist mentor. Eventually he agrees, but only on condition that Paul's proposed "system of documentation" is not translated into English. Paul is too impatient to wait for the two weeks it takes the international postal service to communicate between Brussels and New York, and sends his acceptance of the deal by cablegram.

And now their work is ready for launch. It is opening day, and while Henri schmooses local dignitaries in the hope of raising more funds for the enterprise, Paul sits at the foot of the steep stone Staircase of the Jews, alongside the doors of their new institute, lost in his own thoughts.

Frankly, his grandly-named organisation is not much of an institute, in fact it is a rather run-down and shabby venue, but he is proud of it nonetheless. It occupies one small room measuring three metres by two, which Paul uses as his office. And there is also a gloomy annex filled with row upon row of sliding box files, recycled from a defunct photographer's studio. It currently contains 400,000 index cards, which is in itself a massive achievement and represents a huge amount of work. One day this framework and its content is named The Mundaneum, a name derived from the Latin *mundus* meaning the world and from *aneum* for a place of knowledge. Within the next ten years the number of index cards increases to eleven million, which is the greatest collection of reference material ever assembled in one place.

The little room and its annex are in the Hotel Ravenstein, a dilapidated four hundred year-old mansion in the centre of Brussels. It is the last remaining Gothic building in the city, and although the carcass harks back to the sixteenth century, Paul Otlet's enterprise looks forward to the twentieth.

What Paul sets in motion is a new form of technology using nothing more complex than random-access cards for the mass storage of information. He develops a procedure for the basic functions of computing, the sorting and retrieving of data, and his system is infinitely and continuously expandable. It caters for what a future generation calls "search parameters" which include date, origin, language, subject and content. It also uses the plus sign and the colon mark to establish relationships between these separate items of data. And thanks to Melvil Dewey, the structural coding system is ready-made.

Even in this year of 1895, and even though Paul is cock-a-hoop, the pattern of his future is set, although he does not recognise it. This pattern revolves around money. He is his father's son, always ignoring overambition versus underfunding. The lack of sponsorship and broken promises, versus the awards and the accolades. Great public acclaim, but inevitable commercial failure. Where is the buck in bucking the trend? Where is the profit in prophecy? Where is the box office for a reference library of box files? Instinctively Paul knows that he needs to up his game, but he is learning that knowledge is not always power. What he needs is funding on a scale far greater than anything the Society of Social and Political Sciences is offering.

He falls out with his father, and any thought of asking the Egomaniac for money is out of the question. He confides the circumstances of their falling out to his diary, and it seems to psychologically damage him judging by the number of times he refers to it in the years to come. This is how he tells it.

Father and son meet up at the family estate near *Brussels By Sea* at Westende. Plans are afoot to extend one of the Egomaniac's tram lines to the site, where electrically powered modern villas with sea views can be sited around ornamental gardens, with tennis courts, play areas and a telegraph office for important folk to keep tabs on their business interests. Rules are drawn up for an organisation to make sure the future residents behave themselves and exist in utopian cooperation. Paul is very much taken up by these ideals, but it is always his father who holds the reins.

On this occasion they decamp to an ornate wooden restaurant where the Egomaniac holds forth and Paul is forced to listen but not contribute. The meal proceeds past the bread and oysters, through the pudding and on to the coffee. Then the Egomaniac asks Paul to pass the sugar.

"The sugar bowl is within arm's reach, Father."

"You will kindly pass it to me."

"It is closer to you than it is to me. You can reach for it yourself."

"Are you refusing to pass me the sugar?"

"I am."

"You are a selfish, pig-headed lout!"

"In which case, it must be hereditary."

"I demand that you pass me the sugar!"

"I invite you to go and take a long walk off a short pier."

"This is the last time I will ask, boy. Pass me the sugar now!"

And then to Paul's humiliation and stupefaction, his father flings his coffee cup at Paul, which misses him but hits a perfect stranger at the next table. Paul recalls the scene as he sits alone outside the Hotel Ravenstein. No, he will not ask his father for the time of day, let alone for money. He will have to raise funds for his new organisation elsewhere.

La Fontaine is the man with the contacts, and Paul knows that when it comes to their partnership he is by far the better fundraiser. After all, Henri La Fontaine's cronies in the Senate are responsible for the fact that this *International Federation for Information and Documentation* exists at all, let alone for keeping the project alive. If Paul ever needs to up his game and raise the stakes, then now is the time.

As far as his funders are concerned, Paul's coinage of the term "documentation" only involves the indexing and retrieval of written records. But Paul believes he is ready to reveal his grand scheme of things to them. If his system works for the written content of books, then it works just as well for graphic records, photographs, audio recordings, even moving images, anything and everything with a "documentary" value. And that is where the financial value of all of this lies too.

To set up "offices of information" must have a huge commercial application, just like subscribing to a telephone service and then charging a toll for an individual telephone call. There must be big money to be made from processing data and documentation, but for whom and by when?

He believes that his system can transform any library into an information hub, and he believes that all libraries can be joined together to form a massive information network that reaches beyond the confines of a city, or even the boundaries of a country. What's more, he speculates that such a service can not only be turned into a money machine, but a global industry. His father may have become rich by exploiting his mines and railways, but Paul believes he can become rich by mining information and processing data.

On this day in 1895, sitting on the Staircase of the Jews, Paul Otlet invents the concept of the internet. Before long, he sets about building it. And sooner than later, he succeeds.

Staircase of the Jews, Hotel Ravenstein, 1895

Melvil Dewey, 1895

opening of International Federation for Information and Documentation 1895, Paul Otlet 5th from left

Otlet development site at Westende, 1895

Chapter 6

September 1906
International Institute of Bibliography, 1 Rue de Musée,
Brussels

Robert Goldschmidt is a chemist and an engineer, with a scientific interest in photography. He does not live too far from Paul's grand mansion, within walking distance in fact. Now that the faithful old DuPont studio is gone, Paul is on the look-out for someone from his own generation with whom he can try out his theories, and Goldschmidt fits the bill very well. In a very few years time, Goldschmidt constructs a pioneering transmitter station at Laeken, from where he transmits Europe's first scheduled radio broadcasts, but today he is meeting Paul Otlet at a civilised hour in the International Institute of Blibliography.

It is publication day for their co-authored pamphlet which concerns an ambitious new proposal, a very ambitious new proposal indeed. And what they propose is nothing less than the creation of a global library for all reference books. It is not only global, but it is durable, stable, easy to use, easy to reproduce, portable, and most important of all, it is very cheap. And they reckon they can achieve all of these goals by harnessing a simple invention known as microfilm.

Less than ten years before, the Lumière brothers beam moving pictures to a paying audience for the first time, and now, with the new century only six years old, the Otlet family can enjoy screenings at a cinematic theatre in the Kings Gallery right here in Brussels. Paul embraces the implications of cinema the moment he experiences his first screening, and he is fascinated by the projection device, with its long spool of film that magnifies a stream of tiny images by using light to cast them onto a giant screen.

He experiments with his new collaborator Goldschmidt and together they devise a system which is revolutionary. It is the release of this system that they publish today. Here it is in their own words, translated from the original.

"We hereby declare that traditional books are not the best possible means of storing information, because access to book libraries is not always easy. In fact they delay access to books and discourage even the most tenacious workers, to the detriment of scientific progress.

The need for scholars to travel, the international exchange of scientific books between libraries, copies or extracts requested from abroad, these are all seriously under-resourced. In which case there is a need for a new form of book to overcome such major inconveniences.

What we propose is a solution to this problem that is based on photography, and we have proved beyond any doubt that a single card measuring 12.5 by 7.5 centimetres can contain the contents of an entire book.

The second factor in our proposal is the use of the microphotographic document along with its enlargement, so that it can be read by any user. To be practical, enlargement must be instantaneous and it must be accomplished by the smallest possible device that will not confuse or weary the viewer.

New kinds of apparatus can be created, apart from the simple magnifying glass or the scientific microscope. Illuminated projection is already in use for public entertainment. And not only are detailed scenes projected in laboratories and lecture halls, but microscopic slides are already being projected as well.

If a film-negative is placed in a very simple enlarging machine that contains magnifying glasses and is lit by an electric light, then the image can be enlarged at will to any size, and it can be projected. For example it can be projected on the frosted glass which closes the opposite side of a camera obscura. That is where "seeing" the text and reading it will take place.

A contrivance we have adapted from the carriage of a typewriter can move the image from left to right and from top to bottom merely by pressing two buttons. Thus the reader is free to access the pages that have been microphotographed onto each centimetre of film, one after another, in front of the lens.

If we have the necessary resources at our disposal, all of human thought can be held in a few hundred catalogue drawers, ready for instant access, and to respond to any request. It is quite natural that such developments would seem like marvels of fiction. It is inevitable that at first they would seem to be impossible. That is because the mind will reject any pursuit of them at first. But, according to a common slogan, do we not live in a time in which yesterday's Utopia is today's dream and tomorrow's reality?

So, in order to present tomorrow's dream today, let us simply examine the result of combining microphotography and enlargement by projection, which has already been achieved and is widely used. A roll of motion picture film 50 metres long can now be stored in a little metal box 15 centimetres in diameter and 2.5 centimetres deep. The roll contains 5,000 exposures. Each of these exposures can be projected onto a screen as large as 16 square metres. Therefore, this small canister contains the wherewithal to project eighty-thousand square metres of photographic documents, at will and repeatedly."

Not content with revolutionising data storage on microfilm, Paul goes on to predict the mobile phone and mobile data in this 1906 publication *Les Aspects du Livre*, a full eighty years before the real thing.

"Tomorrow, telephony will be wireless, just like telegraphy. Nobody can stop us from believing this. We will witness a new transformation of the book. Everyone will carry a tiny little handset in his or her pocket, which will be tuned with the turn of a dial to the unique wavelength transmitted by each emitting centre."

 As Paul's words are published, his father Édouard is dying, and what remains of his business empire is falling apart. Paul, his brother Maurice and their five step-siblings form the Otlet Brothers Company. As the eldest, Paul reluctantly becomes president of their new enterprise, which includes the Egomaniac's mines and railways, of which Paul knows next to nothing. His only first-hand experience is in 1900 on a visit with his brother Maurice to accompany their father to the family iron mines in Spanish Moncayo, a desolate place which has the distinction of housing an entire community excommunicated for witchcraft.
 The exploitation of mining is an experience that he loathes, but it is not as loathsome as his memories of the Congolese human zoo, and Paul's first action as President of Otlet Brothers is to get rid of all family interests in the Congo, which he does at a hefty loss. His working life is dominated by proposals to integrate smart indexing and microfilm into his world brain of knowledge, and neither he nor his family are ready, willing or able to cope with his father's legacy. Everyone struggles. It is only a year since Paul beguiles an architect called Octave Van Rysselberghe to develop a tourist resort in the Otlet family hunting grounds in Westende. Inspired by new theories of the Garden City, the project is too much for Paul and it goes off at half-cock. This is a precursor and a warning for his wildly overambitious plans in future years to build a world city. But being his father's son, Paul Otlet is not the type of personality to heed warnings.
 Not long after the Egomaniac dies, a drastic change is precipitated in the Otlet domestic world. Paul and his wife Fernande begin divorce proceedings and a new chapter of his life begins.

the egomaniac Edouard Otlet – memorial photograph

Paul, Maurice & Edouard, centre, at their mines, 1900

Paul Otlet the unwilling businessman, centre, 1906

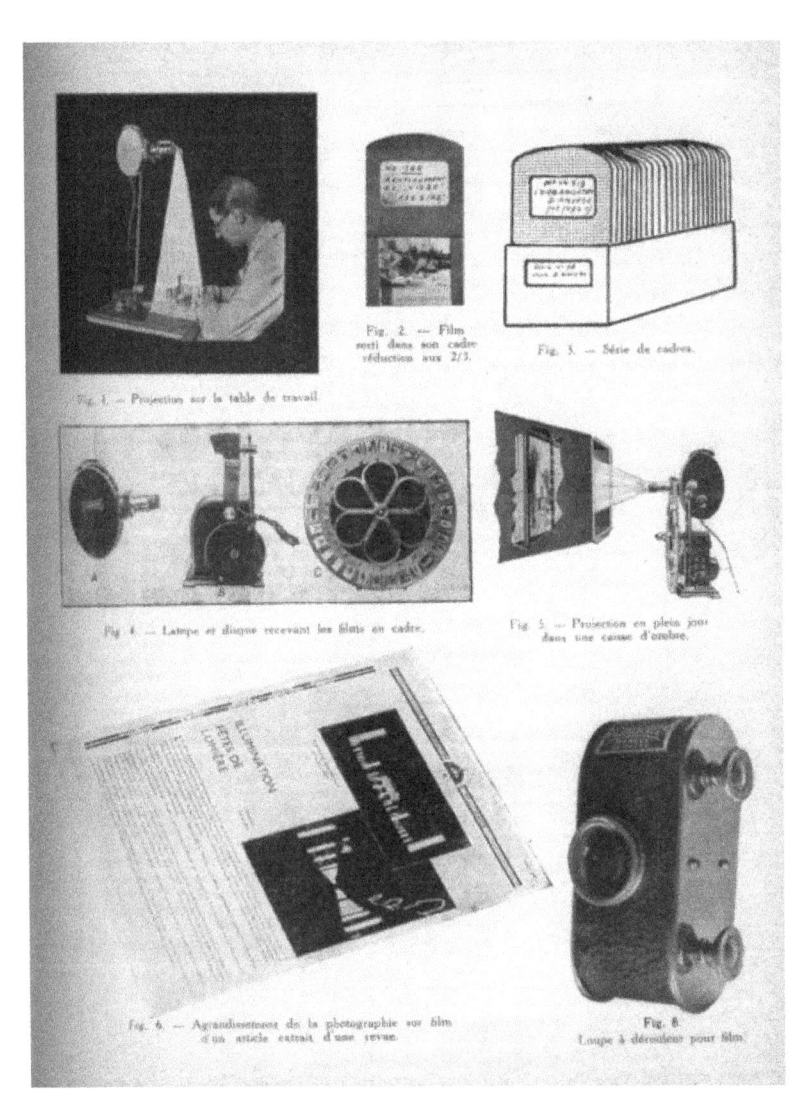

'A New Form of Book – Microphotography'
by Paul Otlet and Robert Goldschmidt, 1906

Chapter 7

June 1907
International Peace Conference, The Hague, Netherlands

Celebrity endorsements work wonders for a brand image, and royal celebrity endorsements can work very well indeed. For example, the British King Edward VII endorses a brand of cigar named after him in exchange for a supply of the smokes that kill him. On the other hand, Leopold II, King of the Belgians, does not endorse cigars but he does endorse the ideas of Paul Otlet and Henri La Fontaine, when he closes the Belgian World Congress in 1905 with the royal proclamation, "Without any need for political ambition, tiny Belgium can become the capital of an important intellectual, artistic, civilising and economic movement, we can be a useful member of the great family of nations and we can contribute our small part to the welfare of humanity."

So when the World Congress concludes that a permanent office needs to be set up to promote His Majesty's notion, Belgium turns to Otlet and La Fontaine's newly formed International Peace Bureau, including their achievements at what they are starting to refer to as "the Mundaneum".

Brussels is already established as a centre for successful international organisations for half a century, and Otlet and La Fontaine are only too happy to help their capital city achieve the King's vision of influence and importance. They snuggle up to the Minister for the Interior and Public Instruction, and use his contacts to assemble a mutual back-slapping network of twenty international associations, all pledged to give one another reciprocal aid, "towards the unification and progressive organisation of the interests of the whole world, as though it is comprised of a single nation above individual nations."

The result of this is the Central Office of International Associations which now includes the Mundaneum as its international centre for documentation and anti-war activities. There is no doubt that things are going well for Paul Otlet and they as set to get even better, because for once he manages to capture the mood of growing international cooperation that peaks at the International Peace Conference in the Hague. It is attended by the leaders of forty-four nations, and it is a showpiece for Henri La Fontaine and Paul Otlet.

Even though the problems under discussion are common to all nations, Paul concludes that there are five distinct groups at this peace conference, and each of these groups is keen to influence the outcome either through the press or through fringe meetings. He believes that the groups are easily identified and lists them as career parliamentarians, lawyers and jurists, ideological socialists, committed pacifists and international associations, and although they all have their own agendas, they have much in common. Paul is forming his own belief system and his own philosophy which influences the remainder of his working life, and which brings about his ultimate frustration, disappointment and failure. But at this stage of the game he is on the up and up.

He understands that communication links are binding these groups closer and closer together, and he foresees that such communications must soon include new technologies as well as the traditional press. He understands that nations are becoming increasingly interdependent, not just economically but in terms of scientific ideas and the arts. He justifies his own belief in a central international university that includes his own system of global indexing and documentation. And he sees this sort of conference becoming a permanent organising body for international associations like his. But as always he includes his dreams as well as his realities. He dreams of an international language, based on codes and cyphers. He dreams of a universal system of weights and measures. And he dreams of a world federation of government with an international parliament.

But back to reality. Paul's first step at his Central Office of International Associations is to compile a directory of all existing international associations. A straightforward task if ever there was one. He then dragoons Cyrille Van Overbergh of the Belgian Sociological Association to send out questionnaires to each of these associations in order to gather eight data points from all of them. These data points are their identity, their history, how they classify themselves, how they were formed, how they function, how they have evolved, how they can be disbanded, and finally their bibliographic and other resources.

An important source for Paul's initial listing of existing associations is the *Annuaire de la Vie Internationale* published over the previous two years by the International Institute for Peace at Monaco by a fellow compulsive cataloguer named Alfred Fried. Paul contacts him and pitches him with a snapshot of his vision. Fried agrees to join forces and they pool their resources. The next edition of the *Annuaire* is jointly edited by Fried, La Fontaine and Otlet himself, and it is funded by several international institutions dragooned by La Fontaine. The result is a huge publication, running to over a thousand pages, and it is hailed as a great success by the international community. Unfortunately, the international community is at the root of Paul's greatest problem.

To get government funding, Paul's organisation has to be recognised as a *personnification civile*, that is to say it must be recognised as a legal entity in Belgium. Without this recognition it cannot own property, enter into contracts, receive financial donations, or do all the things that it needs to do in order to expand and succeed. But this legal recognition is never properly resolved, and Paul simply ignores it and skates along regardless. With the Mundaneum in full swing and as Paul launches the expanded Central Office of International Associations, the future seems bright. But events are already unfolding to ensure that the brightness can not last very long. Europe is changing, King Edward will soon be dead, Tsar Nicholas is divorced from reality and the Kaiser is bipolar. Meanwhile, in a suburb of Bremen, a little boy named Hans Hagemeyer gets upset when he is told he will soon be going to big school.

logo and organisational diagram of the Central Office of International Associations, 1907

International Peace Conference, The Hague, 1907

Chapter 8

November 1910
The Brussels International Exposition, Belgium

This is the high spot in the career of Paul Otlet, a period when he is flourishing, happy, successful, prosperous, well-supported and famous. It all comes crashing down with the outbreak of the Great War, but the outbreak of the Great War is four years in the future, and for now Paul can make his grand plans and bask in the approval of the great and the good.

When he plans to hold an international peace congress in San Francisco sooner than later, he is supported by the American Secretary of State who says the USA gladly welcomes "any international agreement which your government supports regarding your organisation."

When Paul asks his own Belgian government authorities for more space and more money to extend his International Exposition in the *Palais du Cinquantenaire*, the Minister for Arts and Sciences responds, "My dear Paul, I am hastening to get you support from my colleagues in the Public Works department to expedite your request."

When the Spanish Count of Torre-Velez wangles Paul a gong as Commander of the Civil Order of Alfonso XII, it represents "the principal Spanish decoration awarded for personal merit, carrying the appellation *Illustrissimo Senor*."

When Andrew Carnegie, born into Scottish poverty and now the richest man in the world, visits Paul's International Museum, he is "astonished at what I find and never has a visit given me so much pleasure at the revelation of what I find and the importance of the work of the international association." Carnegie's most famous saying is, "The man who dies rich dies disgraced." Whereas Paul Otlet, who is born into Belgian wealth and privilege, is better labelled by the saying, "The way for a rich man to make a small fortune is to start with a large fortune."

The Brussels International Exposition opens on the 23rd of April 1910 and runs until the first day of November. Immediately after it closes Paul is given permission to combine an international library, an international museum, an international university, a central hub for official international institutions and his ever-expanding data service. Soon all of these services and institutes are homed on a grand scale in the *Palais du Cinquantenaire* exactly as he had anticipated when he first took his young sons to view the human zoo there. The cost of setting everything up is a massive half a million francs, paid for by the Belgian Government, and Paul takes it upon himself to officially rename the expanded Palace Mondial as the Mundaneum.

His new mission-control is on a scale far beyond his wildest dreams. As well as the grand entrance hall and wide circulation areas, the layout runs to eighteen rooms for administration offices, four great auditoriums, five bibliographic centres, another nine rooms for the international library, thirty-five galleries for international museums and seven university study hubs. The funding also allows Paul to include two information centres, two massive chambers for the data-processing of sixteen million searchable cards, a dedicated telephone and telegraph complex, a restaurant and a smoking room.

As always, Henri La Fontaine plays an important part in getting the public on side as well as the Government. As soon as the money comes through for his Nobel Peace Prize, he donates the funds to the Mundaneum and makes sure that it is featured heavily in his prize citation. The publicity is great, and it soon attracts extra funding from Belgian investors and philanthropists. Theodore Marburg, the American Representative to Brussels is mightily impressed, and he writes letters of introduction to the US Congress on behalf of Paul, who boards the trans-Atlantic steamship to visit members of the US Government on a fund-raising campaign for the Mundaneum. But when the clouds of war begin to gather on the European horizon, the Americans get cold feet, and Paul returns home empty handed. He does not foresee that this is the shape of things to come. From now on restrictions on funding mean that the Mundaneum can never expand again, and in the real world, the dream is over. But in Paul's world he simply fails to wake up to reality until it is too late.

Mundaneum team

Mundaneum data-processing

Mundaneum telegraph room

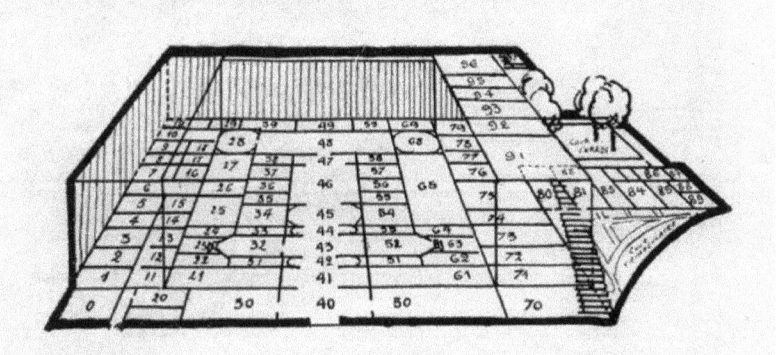

DISTRIBUTION DES SALLES

1. Administration et Offices des Associations Internationales : Salles 1 à 18.
2. Congrès Internationaux, grand auditoire et salle de réception : Salles 28, 43, 48, 68.
3. Institut International de Bibliographie : Salles 7 à 9; 46 et 47.
4. Bibliothèque Internationale : Salles 51 à 54; 61 à 65.
5. Encyclopédie documentaire : Salles 35 à 37.
6. Musée International : Salles 21 à 33; 50; 70 à 99.
7. Université Internationale : Salles 19, 29, 38, 39, 49, 58, 59.
8. Services auxiliaires, Hall d'entrée, indicateur des services : Salles 40 et 41; Postes et Télégraphes : Salle 30; Restaurant, fumoir : Salles 98 et 99. Librairie des Associations : étage, aile droite.

Mundaneum floor plan

63

Mundaneum micro-photography exhibition room

Chapter 9

June 1912
Bauwens Notary Office, Brussels, Belgium

The people who turn Paul's dreams into reality, the workers who run the show, the personnel who maintain the hardware, who populate the databases, who keep it all going, these people are predominantly women. They are the women who are engaged to run the Mundaneum not because they are drudges or subservient or even cheap, but because they are dedicated, loyal, and very clever. One, always formally known as Mademoiselle Poels, is especially important, acting as Paul's long-term factotum. Another woman, Marie-Louise de Bauche, is equally important, not least because she has superb organisational skills and the ability to exist without sleep.

But there are three other women, without whom Paul Otlet's story cannot exist, and without whom his *Palais Mondial* and the Mundaneum cannot come into being. The first of this female trio is the fearsome Léonie La Fontaine, the sister of Paul's great friend Henri. The second is the brilliant Mathilde La Fontaine, the wife of Paul's great friend Henri. And the third is his own wife, the beautiful soul who is Cato Van Nederhesselt, and she turns out to be the love of Paul Otlet's life.

True love? Paul, the unblinking visionary, the divorced failure, can he reveal another side to his character? It seems that the answer to this question is yes, and our man turns out to be a romantic after all. Today is the day that he marries Cato Van Nederhesselt at Bauwens Notary Office, and from this day onwards they remain together until the day Paul dies. He writes private love letters to his inamorata. How deep is his love? It seems very deep. Here is a glimpse of this love in his own words.

"Cato, Catoeje, Catoejeke. These are your three names that I whisper softly. One for each moment, one for each mood, growing one into the next, because the first grows into the third and the second grows from the first, three soft strokes of my bow, three stroked strings of your harp, and here we are together. Listen, listen to the echo of your infinite harmonies. We need this, our begging arms demand this, and the moon and the sun and the sea and the stars, and all that is, and more, and you, and me, and ourselves."

Their marriage certificate shows that the bride's full name is Catherine Gérardine Antoinette Marie van Nederhasselt, she is four years older than the groom and she comes from Amsterdam. It also states that the groom's full name is Paul Joseph Marie Ghislain Otlet, a divorcee whose former wife is dead.

His new wife Cato is not only beautiful, she is also extremely wealthy, a fact that plays a significant part in Paul's future ambitions and his overambitions. Cato is first introduced to Paul by Leonie La Fontaine a few days after his divorce comes through, and she seems genuinely interested in his work to the extent that she declares to Henri, Leonie and Paul himself that she would love to be part of it.

The witness to the marriage of Paul and Cato is the 58-year-old lawyer named on the marriage certificate as Henri La Fontaine. Ever present, ever faithful, ever supportive. Historians, academics and computer nerds cannot deny that Paul Otlet benefits hugely from basking in the reflected glory of the world-famous Henri La Fontaine. Without Henri and without his reputation and achievements, Paul may well only achieve a fraction of his legacy. What is also undeniably true is that Henri La Fontaine hugely benefits from being married to the force of nature that is Mathilde Lhoest. Without her and without her reputation and without her achievements, Henri may well only achieve a fraction of his legacy in turn. And so it can be argued that the fact the Mundaneum ever exists at all can be traced back to the powerhouse that is Mathilde.

Henri and Mathilde marry back in 1903. Henri is an unusual match. He is 49 years old, a bachelor, a lawyer, a Freemason and a very fine pianist. But he is also her intellectual equal and they spark off one another like binary stars. They do not have children. They remain devoted to one another. They die at a ripe old age only a few months apart, embracing two world wars and one Nobel Peace Prize. But if Henri and Mathilde La Fontaine play a vital part in the story of the Mundaneum, it is nowhere near as vital as the part played by Henri's sister Léonie.

Léonie La Fontaine is a remarkable pioneer of both pacifism and feminism. She is a founder member of the Belgian League for the Rights of Women, the National Belgian Womens Council and the Belgian League for Peace and Freedom. She is in the thick of it when it comes to the Mundaneum's foundation and fundraising, she helps with Paul's publications on documentation, in fact she launches the Central Office of Feminine Documentation the year before the Mundaneum opens its doors. Léonie la Fontaine builds a network of very powerful ladies, and her Belgian League for the Rights of Women pushes the cause for women to be accepted into the professions. She mocks every convention by exploiting and subverting social fashion events, and her Happy Hour drinks parties are a hotbed of revolution. But Belgium will lag behind the rest of Europe when it comes to giving women the right to vote. That does not happen until 1949, the year Léonie dies, and neither Mathilde La Fontaine nor Cato Otlet live long enough to enjoy that right.

A few short months after Paul and Cato's wedding, their witness Henri La Fontaine is recognised as "the effective leader of the peace movement in Europe" and awarded the Nobel Peace Prize "for his unparalleled contribution to the organisation of peaceful internationalism." But Henri is under no illusions whatsoever. "Peoples will be as before," he says, "sheep sent to the slaughterhouses or to the meadows, at the whim of the shepherds." A few short months later The War To End All Wars breaks out, and the role of women in the workplace changes forever.

The start of the First World War delivers a double personal tragedy for Paul. In less than one hundred days from its outbreak his older son Marcel is taken as a prisoner of war by the Germans, and all contact is lost. Then his younger son Jean goes missing in the carnage that is the Battle of the Yser river in Flanders. Not knowing if Jean is dead or wandering shellshocked in the mud, and in spite of Cato pleading for him not to risk his own life, Paul waits for a lull in the fighting to go to the battlefield himself and search for his boy's body. This is the pivotal decision in his commitment to peace. It is not confirmed that his younger son is dead for another two years, when his elder son Marcel finds written evidence while still in a prisoner of war camp.

When the Germans occupy Brussels, Paul's new wife agrees they should flee the country, first to her family home in Holland and then across the North Sea to England. Paul is unhappy with this temporary exile, and from there they head back across the English Channel to France and on to the neutrality of Switzerland. Paul now goes into overdrive with anti-war publications, and even before he quits Brussels he publishes *La Fin de la Guerre*, The End Of War, where he sets out the framework for a World Charter of Human Rights and an international community of federal states. This is the beginning of what is to become the League of Nations. Paul dedicates the publication to his two sons, and also to Albert, King of the Belgians, who sends a warm personal acknowledgement in writing.

From the neutral safety on the shores of Lake Geneva, Paul chairs the *Conférence des Nationalités* in Lausanne, and as a result voices are raised that accuse him of being a German sympathiser, but this is a nonsense and Cato defends him against all-comers as she helps Paul edit his statement to the world. Here is Paul's text.

"At the beginning of the twentieth century, mankind experiences a world that none of our ancestors has ever known. Deep economic transformations due to the constant progress of technology, generated themselves by wonderful scientific discoveries, multiply production tenfold, proportionally broaden consumption and distribute wealth more accurately in all social strata.

The sophisticated means of transport and communication circulate people, goods and ideas. They open up a global market for us all, and transform the intellectual and social order. Internationalised science is now as broad a field as religion. The arts take on the task of improving existence. Spirits are being educated and freed. The conception of life is made both more realistic and more idealistic. The obligations of morality extend ever-wider.

Suddenly this monstrous war comes to pit the flood of its brutalities against this ascent to a world civilization. Thirteen nations are fighting against each other, each claiming that it is for their own survival. Twenty million soldiers are under arms. War on land, war by dreadnoughts, submarines and floating mines, war in the air. The combined armies of Genghis Khan, Timur, Xerxes, Hannibal, Caesar, Saladin and Napoleon are dwarfed compared to those fighting now. 200 million francs of wealth destroyed every day, 3 million square miles vandalised by the most sophisticated war machines. The treasures accumulated by centuries of work at the mercy of bombs. Trade is in chaos, industries, agriculture, the arts and the sciences are paralysed. There are more victims already than in all the wars added up in history since the Flood.

All nations arriving at a certain stage are condemned to renew or to perish. The world today is a chrysalis. International and national reforms will emerge from the crisis, imposing a new mentality, a new order, dissociating ourselves from a finite past, breaking from old designs and old organizations. And if, on the contrary, this war is not to make such a revolution triumph, all these ruins, all these sufferings, all these dead will have served no purpose. Old life will resume with a misjudged and ill-conceived peace. Instead of being 'the last war' as we would surely want, this war may turn out to be the first in a whole series."

A number of influential voices start to be raised against Paul because he is not as rabidly anti-German as his fellow countrymen. This notion is misconceived, of course. He is rabidly anti-war in all its forms. But the voices first whisper that he is disloyal to his Belgian brethren and then grow louder, accusing him of being a traitor to the allies. This is nonsense, but when steps are taken to deny him going to Paris, he is forced to write a letter to Monsieur Durand, the Prefect of Police there, and this is what he says.

"I have come to Paris to make propaganda for peace, but like any normal man who thinks and reflects, I am completely preoccupied by the origins of this war, and by what should follow it. I have given myself over to the study of these questions in order to be able at last to find some objective basis for them, which is required for the solution of any problem according to scientific methods.

Towards this goal, I have consulted personalities in the worlds of science and politics, long standing acquaintances for the most part, and I have given a course of five lectures at the School of Advanced Social Studies called *After the War*. I have taught at this School before the war, and the course was as much requested by the Administration as urged on by me. For twenty years, the study of international questions has been one of my occupations. I founded in Brussels with the patronage and material support of the Belgian government, the Union of International Associations, which attempted to concentrate and co-ordinate the international movement of which Belgium had spontaneously become the headquarters fifty years ago. I am one of the originators of the great Congresses of this Union. I direct its office and publications as well as its Museum, set up in State buildings.

In other words, I am an internationalist. I will add that I am not a pacifist. The distinction, which is not always made, is a valid one. At the same time that the means of communication make the world smaller and smaller, the population which lives in it is growing larger and larger. It follows that it is impossible to keep each group in its own territory. International contacts are established and multiply, and there is a two-fold result. On the one hand interests become established beyond political frontiers, every one being more or less involved in the universal circulation of men, products and ideas. On the other hand, antagonisms multiply along with the points of contact, and the spheres of friction grow larger. As a rule, governments have not been sufficiently aware of this profound transformation. As a result, all of this international life, both so fertile and so dangerous, has been left almost completely to its own devices, rather than being framed in institutions which could give it organisation and establish necessary checks and balances.

It is necessary to search out the deep causes, not of this war (there have always been wars) but of the universal character of this war, of its implications, direct and indirect, for every element of the civilian population.

The pacifist wants peace at any price. His feelings delude him about human goodness and do not lead him to reason about sociological causes. Internationalism itself is waiting for a lasting peace, for a better organisation of relations between peoples, of which it would be the mature fruit. Peace at any price, peace without justice, peace today without surety that it will persist tomorrow, cannot concern it.

The evil which should be done away with is international insecurity, an evil that made its ravages felt long before the war itself, for the armed peace, with its continual alerts, was really latent war, and prevented the foundation of anything stable.

Internationalists consider that, in the future, security should be demanded for the organisation of a Society of Nations after the same fashion in which national security has been organised. There should be a common power to decide what it is necessary to do in this domain, a Justice to which all conflicts are compulsorily submitted, an executive body enforcing sanctions, worldwide and economic in the first stage and military in the last stage, forming an international allied army. The Society of Nations should be founded on liberty and equality.

These opinions agree deeply with my patriotic faith, for the interests of Belgium are linked to the final triumph of these principles. It is for its liberty, for the honour of its given word, for the cause of its violated rights, that my country has accepted its martyrdom. It is because of this that my two sons, my only children, have gone to fight. The younger, voluntarily enlisted with my consent, has been reported missing in the Battle of the Yser. If this war should not end in the establishment of a stable Society of Nations, all of our sacrifices will have been in vain."

Cato Van Nerderhesselt Otlet

Mathilde La Fontaine

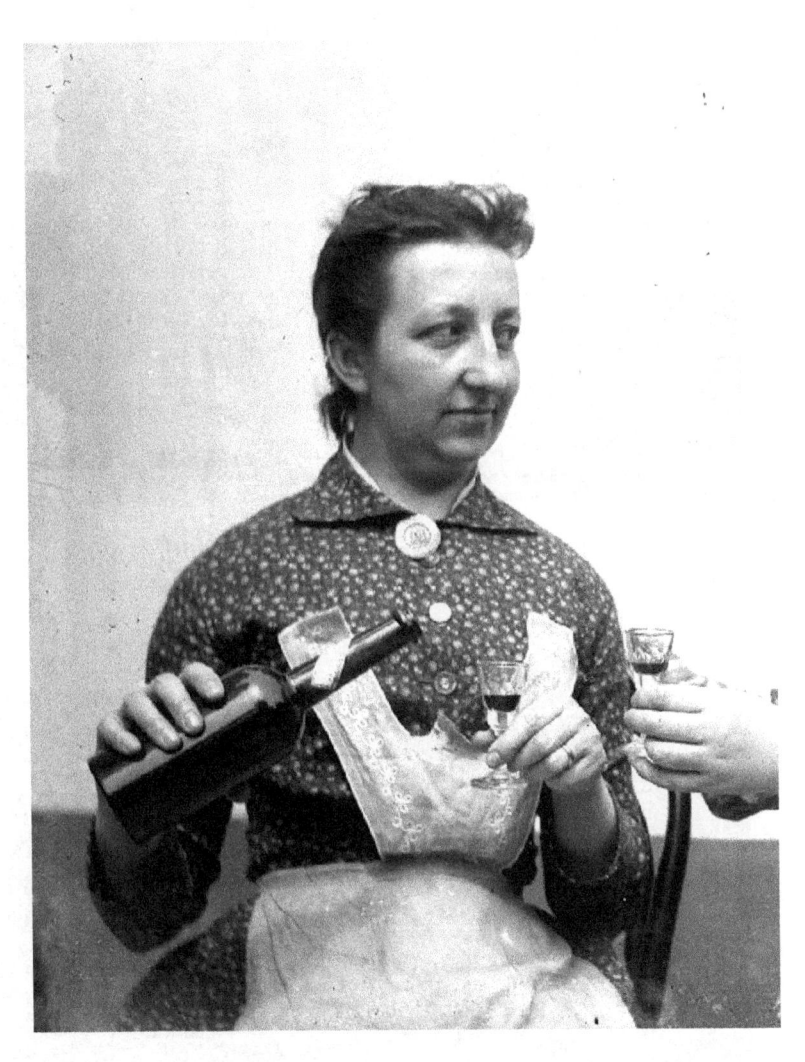

Léonie La Fontaine, Happy Hour

Léonie La Fontaine, far right, and her political allies

Mademoiselle Poels at work in the Mundaneum

Marie-Louise de Bauche at work in the Mundaneum

Poels, de Bauche and Mundaneum assistants

King Albert of Belgium and Queen Elizabeth of Bavaria visit the Yser front, 1914, where Paul searches for his son Jean

Chapter 10

September 1921
The Mundaneum, Brussels

"Hello?"
"Allo?"
"Is this the line for the Mundaneum information service in Brussels, Belgium?"
"Parlez-vous Français, monsieur? You are English? You are American?"
"Um, no madame. I am Jamaican."
"Jamais con!"
"I am from Jamaica."
"Veuillez patienter un instant, Monsieur. Je vais chercher quelqu'un qui parle anglais. Un moment. Un moment, s'il vous plaît."
"..."
"Yes, hello Sir. My name is Mademoiselle Poels, who is this please?"
"Hello Madame, Madamoiselle. My name is Marcus Garvey."
"Yes. Monsieur Marcus. How can we help for you today, monsieur?"
"I am the founder of the Universal Negro Improvement Association."
"Yes, monsieur."
"I am the Provisional President of Africa."
"Quoi?"
"I am telephoning you from Harlem in New York, United States."
"Yes, monsieur."
"I am told by Mister William Du Bois that your documentation service can supply instant information on every topic in the world. Is that right?"

"Information? Oui, that is correct. Do you have the Mundaneum account, monsieur?"

"Mister W.E.B Du Bois is in charge of a conference at your Palace Mondial at the end of this month. He is a personal friend of Mister Paul Otlet."

"Monsieur Otlet is my employer, yes. You would like to open the personal account with us, Sir?"

"Do you have an information system that can deliver information by wire?"

"Information by wire? Ah, le télégraphe. Oui, that is correct. What is it you wish to know, monsieur?"

"I would like you to tell me the names and organisation details of every Negro leader in the world, and all the names and organisation details of organisations fighting for negro rights and slavery compensation."

"Monsieur? Organisations for Negro rights?"

"Can you do that?"

"Of course. We have every information. You wish information to be delivered by the telegraph?"

"Yes, yes. How long will it take to gather everything and wire me the information?"

"One moment, Sir. I check my *calendrier*. But you have to open the personal account with us."

"How long will it take you to wire all the information to me in New York?"

"Environ, erm, my estimation is, ah, thirty-six minutes, monsieur."

The Mundaneum telegraph room has sixteen workstations, set out in two parallel banks of eight. Data is transmitted by wire and remote output is printed out on tickertape to any capable receiver in the world. The millions of data cards are held in rank after rank of sliding box files, and indexed to perfection by Paul and his team. The operatives are so used to retrieving information on-demand that they hardly need to consult the location indices to find the relevant filing cabinet, categories, sliding drawer and individual data card.

The Belgian conference event that interests Marcus Garvey is the Second Pan-African Congress which is organised by William Du Bois, pioneer of the American civil rights movement, and hosted by Paul Otlet at the *Palais Mondial*. It is Paul's intention to stage a glittering reception for delegates in the fifteenth century Bruxelles Hôtel de Ville, and the rumours of extravagance that reach Marcus Garvey trigger his phone call. Garvey intends to make his feelings known to all potential delegates, and he intends to use the resources of the Mundaneum itself to achieve his aim. His feelings are distinctly uneasy.

The Brussels Pan-African conference follows a recent event in Paris, sponsored by the American National Association for the Advancement of Coloured People, and Marcus Garvey considers such expensive overseas ventures do nothing but divert funds away from his true struggle at home in America. He sees William Du Bois as an apologist, and Paul Otlet as an opportunist, and he believes that because the Pan-African Congress lacks any official status it will do more harm than good.

The list of movers and shakers that are the potential delegates, as disgorged by the Mundaneum data files, is stiff with diplomats, lawyers, politicians, military officers, business moguls, and what Du Bois calls the "talented tenth". These are held in a list of educated black leaders and assorted high-profile black men and women of influence and money. Advance press coverage refers to them as "an imposing gathering of men and women, all of whom stand out for diplomacy, for scholarship and for intelligence." The official press release of the Second Pan-African Congress calls them the "intellectual efflorescence of the Negro race". Marcus Garvey begs to differ.

Thirty-two nations are "represented" and highlighted on a huge map that decorates the main conference room. There is also a massive painting of Prometheus stealing fire from the gods, used as a stage backdrop. Over two thousand visitors, journalists and observers attend the Pan-African conference sessions, but Paul is heavily criticised for trying to hijack the Congress to promote the interests of the Mundaneum. Not to mention an ambition to promote his own plans for a World City.

After the event, Marcus Garvey contacts as many people and organisations on the list as he can, in order to make his opinion absolutely clear.

"The Congress has been a select gathering of personally invited and self-appointed delegates, which have been compiled akin to an exclusive university function, to an assembly dance or a pink tea affair."

He accuses the Congress of being a staged performance of respectability, and says of Du Bois and Otlet that even though they might "put the Congress delegates up in the best hotels, that does not make them legitimate representatives of black voices." They are "merely a group of hand-picked delegates selected and invited by Doctor Du Bois, and they are mostly job-holders under imperialist governments, tourists, and white liberals."

For the time being, Paul is unaffected by the rebuke, but the Brussels authorities who indirectly fund the Congress begin to have doubts about his motives as well as his judgement. Those with longer memories wonder if the son is taking after his egomaniac father in terms of pig headedness, wilfulness and self-aggrandisement.

Two years later, when state funding of the Mundaneum comes under question, Paul takes great satisfaction in trashing the opinions and reputation of Marcus Garvey, who is convicted of mail fraud and imprisoned in the US Penitentiary of Atlanta. Two years after that Garvey's reputation is in tatters when he is investigated by the FBI and deported from the United States, never to return.

Marcus Garvey, 1924

William Du Bois, 1921

Second Pan-African Congress, Palais Mondial, 1921

Pan-African Congress delegates with Paul Otlet, extreme left, and Henri La Fontaine, centre, 1921

Chapter 11

December 1924
The Mundaneum, Brussels, Belgium

After Paul Otlet officially renames his *Palais Mondial* the Mundaneum, he begins work on an insanely grand project for a *Cité Mondiale*, a global city to act as the centre for world peace, industry, science, fine arts, religion and commerce.

Cité Mondiale, the World City or Universal City, is a concept that Paul Otlet works on over the same number of years as Adolf Hitler is involved with a similar grand scheme for his *Germania* World City, and with the same miserable lack of success.

Paul extends his theories for global cooperation into the physical world, and he tries to involve several architects sympathetic to the idea of a city of knowledge, to bring humans together and put an end to wars. Paul's dream of a global centre for "harmonious, peaceful and progressive civilisation" is shared by an American sculptor called Hendrik Christian Anderson, but after years of frustration and zero progress, Anderson eventually turns to the Italian dictator Mussolini for funding to build the city. Of course Paul walks away in disgust at the prospect of such an alliance.

Then, in a similar way that he uses the reputation of Henri La Fontaine to advance the Mundaneum, Paul now uses his beloved Cato to harness the reputation of the world-famous architect Le Corbusier to endorse the idea of a *Cité Mondiale*, and she persuades the great man to draw up grandiose plans. Paul and Cato hawk the concept to the City of Brussels without success, and get the same negative reaction from councils in Geneva, Antwerp, Rome and Washington. As ever, Paul seems undaunted and maintains his blind determination in the face of repeated rejection. Why would these great cities not want to fund his plans for a World City, complete with a World Museum, a World University, a World Library, an Olympic Centre, Embassies for every nation on Earth, and of course a global Mundaneum. To which the answer is, they simply cannot afford it.

It can be argued that in several aspects of his beliefs, Paul Otlet is divorced from reality. For example, he forms a friendship with the painter Jean Delville, who is a spiritualist, occult dabbler, theosophist and follower of a messianic prophet figure named Krishnamurti. It is Delville's huge painting of the myth of *Promethée* that decorates the Mundaneum conference room, and is created to help viewers see the revealed light of the Great Truth. There is the time when Paul goes to an encampment in Holland and gives a lengthy sermon to several thousand members of the Order Of The Star Of The East, which is where he meets Krishnamurti, the Great Truth Giver himself, for conversations about the nature of love, peace, an end to all wars and of course the Mundaneum.

The designs for the World City and the Mundaneum itself have definite occultist symbolism. Le Corbusier's drawings are based on Paul's original concepts, which echo the observatory of the ancient Assyrian palace of Khorsabad, in the form of a stepped pyramid with spiral access ramps. The Czech writer and critic Karel Tiege calls these designs for the Mundaneum "an expression of ideological and metaphysical imagination" and "a place of worship for idols and gods."

Sacred or profane, Paul's architectural dreams are occupying too much of his time, and he takes his eye off the ball when it comes to protecting the future of the Mundaneum. The very first sign of trouble happens here and now in 1924, but it goes almost unnoticed by Paul. The Belgian government decides to stage a trade fair for the rubber industry, in order to show off the wonders of modern industrialisation alongside advances in their colonial rubber plantations.

There are those in the Brussels local government who still remember the kudos that the great exhibition at the old Colonial Palace brought them twenty-five years before, and they look towards the site of what is now the *Palais Mondial* and the Mundaneum to recreate former glories. Surely Monsieur Otlet would not mind giving up a few rooms on a temporary basis to make way for a Rubber Fair.

Monsieur Otlet has other things on his mind. He ignores the threat and the rooms are commandeered. This single act of Paul's wilful neglect marks the start of a series of questions regarding value for money by the government, and they begin to question the public funds they allocate to this self-declared Mundaneum. It is the beginning of the end. In ten years time it will lead to the withdrawal of all funding, and leave Paul high and dry.

Cité Mondial concept, Paul Otlet and Hendrik Christian Anderson

Paul (centre) Mathilde & Henri (right) outside the Palais Mondial

Cité Mondial planners
Le Corbusier centre, and Paul Otlet right

Chapter 12

7 July 1931
Palais Mondial, Brussels, Belgium

The *Palais Mondial*, affectionately known as the Mundaneum, created by the determination of Paul Otlet and Henri La Fontaine as a centre of world peace through knowledge, is twenty years old today. The rooms that once buzzed with activity are mostly silent. If Paul does wander among the millions of files that fester there, he does it alone and without any real purpose.

And so it is that today is different. It is the day that the venue hosts a Universal Peace Congress, attended by many of the great and the good, but to be truthful it is not attended by that many of either. Paul uses the occasion to issue what he calls his *Belgian Appeal to the World*. It is his warning to humanity that unless action is taken right now, the nations of the world are on course to destroy one another. The timing is critical. Tomorrow is the opening of the International Disarmament Conference, a multi-national talking shop that goes on for two years and ends in total failure.

The style of Paul's prose is flowery and probably overwritten, but it is personal, anguished and brutally honest. Just after noon, on Tuesday July 7th 1931, on the day the Communist Party newspaper *The Red Flag* is banned in Berlin, on the day *All Quiet On The Western Front* is banned from German libraries, on the day three former British Prime Ministers compose a joint plea for disarmament, Paul Otlet makes his appeal to the world. These are his words, translated afresh.

"Nations of the earth, O World, in the tumult of recent events listen to the voice of Belgium! Little Belgium who, after eighty-four years of peace and uninterrupted labour, awoke one morning in 1914 to a Europe in flames, and for the next four years was a martyr to what followed. In 1918 reparation and security were promised to Belgium. Above all there was the promise that Belgium would never undergo this terrible experience again, and that such terror would never recur anywhere else.

And now, in 1931, all that Belgium hears are the agitated sounds of artillery and the drone of aircraft on training flights. All that she smells are the experiments being undertaken with gas. And now a war of economics has followed the political war, and Belgium is shaken by the crisis that has overtaken her as it has her neighbours. All that she hears are rumours of revolution, the echoes of confusion near at hand and of upheavals far off.

O World, hear my sorrow! It arises as much from fear and uncertainty as from evils already suffered. Where are you going? Towards what destiny do you lead us? How much longer will you leave everything to chance? My nation has done nothing, wanted to take nothing, to destroy nothing, so must my martyrdom begin again on the secular battlefield of Europe, a slaughter-house of peoples. Must I be destroyed again. Having given my sons, must I now give my grandsons?

Opposing camps have set up immense war machines. Activating them needs only the smallest trigger, smaller than the energy needed to throw a switch. To live with these new war machines is terrifying. They transform existence into a nightmare. One mistake, one misunderstanding, one misjudgement, one criminal intention, and immediately all the gears of the war machine begin to engage, snatching up our precious possessions, inflicting grievous wounds, everywhere seizing the ideals that have been declared to be sacred, because without them life was thought to be not worth living.

What must be done, O World? Let me tell you. First our state of mind must be transformed. War must be rooted out of our thoughts. It must be rooted out of any of the institutions whose hearts it has touched. This requires a gigantic effort, a renewal of life and civilization, the overturning of an economic system, which if it does not expressly desire war, at least it leads to war.

We are now compelled to seek a rational and peaceful revolution in order to avoid its violent and chaotic alternative. But any revolution is only the manifestation of a state of mind in the mass of a people. Once its ideas for peace have been formulated they must then be disseminated to influence public opinion. It is necessary to embody these ideas in five essential points that can be listed as follows.

One. We must enforce the judgments of the International Court of Justice by means of sanctions imposed by a World Police Force to counterbalance the individual forces in the armed hands of threatening states.

Two. We must replace the present arbitrariness by the stable framework of a World Constitution extended by an immediate code of international law.

Three. We must use unrestricted admission to replace the current Assembly at Geneva, in which only governments are represented, by a World Parliament that is representative of the peoples and the interests of the whole world.

Four. We must give all the elements of international life the means of communicating with each other in a World Hub which will function as a permanent home for associations and will express the oneness of mankind.

Five. Finally, guaranteed and supported by these global institutions, we must develop a complete World Plan that coordinates all plans into one, and thereby prevents the nations exhausting themselves by pulling in different directions while thinking that they are working toward their own good, which risks bringing about general warfare.

Peoples of the world, do you, like me, wish for Peace? Hear my cry of anguish. Respond to this appeal. Without wasting an hour let us at last offer to mankind the Organisation that it awaits. Founded on a Constitution and directed by a Plan, such an organisation will simultaneously bring about on Earth the conditions for and the rights of Universal Civilisation: Liberty, Justice and Prosperity, and with them Boundless Progress."

Fine words, but it is too late. One week later, the German banking system collapses and the road to disaster begins.

Paul Otlet, Mundaneum 20th anniversary portrait

Paul Otlet, alone in the Mundaneum

Henri La Fontaine and Paul Otlet (central),
Universal Peace Congress, 7 July 1931

Collapse of the German banking system
13 July 1931

Chapter 13

22 May 1934
Cultural Centre, Antwerp, Belgium

A man steadies himself and holds on to the wooden handrail as he climbs up the three wide steps to the lectern. The room is too dark. Paul is now sixty-six years old and gives this same lecture several times since the Mundaneum shut its doors, closed down by order of the government after the final withdrawal of funds. Each time he delivers his rallying cry for a world-wide network of information and knowledge, the audience seems smaller, less interested, more preoccupied by events across the border in Germany and the latest rantings of the madman Hitler who has been in power there for less than a year.

Paul peers ahead, strokes his soft, white beard and adjusts his frameless glasses. Particles of dust dance in the electric beam that pins him to the backcloth like a laboratory specimen. He coughs into his hand. His wife Cato is in the front row, and she motions with her handkerchief for him to dab his chin.

"Distinguished guests." He coughs again, and obediently dabs his chin.

"I believe you know who I am, and I believe you know that our beloved resource of knowledge and information will continue to fall into disrepair unless alternative funding is forthcoming. But as the unthinkable happens before our eyes, all is far from lost. In fact I see it as an opportunity not to rebuild the past, but to lay the foundations for the future."

Some members of the audience shift uncomfortably. They fear that Paul is going to ask them directly for donations, here and now. But he is not. He is going to speak clearly and succinctly and deliver a message from the heart, as he always does. Here is the exact transcription of his opening text, translated from the French. He begins again, like this.

"Distinguished guests. We are where we are, and now what we must do is to move on. And what we must do is to assemble a collection of machines which can perform the following operations, simultaneously or sequentially. What I am talking about is machines that can deliver seven individual operations which must be performed together. Let me list them for you.

Operation number One - the transformation of sound into writing.

Operation number Two - the reproduction of this writing into as many copies as are needed.

Operation number Three - the creation of data in such a way that each item of information has its own identity, and in its relationships with other items comprising any collection of data, can be retrieved as necessary.

Operation number Four - a classification number assigned to each specific item of information.

Operation number Five - the automatic classification and filing of this data by machine.

Operation number Six - the automatic retrieval of data for consultation, presented either direct to the enquirer or via machine, enabling written additions to be made.

And finally, operation number Seven - the mechanical manipulation at will of all the listed items of information, in order to obtain new combinations of facts, new relationships of ideas, and new operations carried out with the help of numeric code.

The technology fulfilling these seven requirements will create a mechanical collective brain.

All information must be condensed so that it can be contained on a personal desk, within hand's reach, and indexed in such a way as to ensure maximum accessibility.

In this case, the world described in the entirety of all knowledge will be within everyone's grasp. A Universal Book.

The Universal Book created from all books will become an annex to the brain, a substratum of memory, an external mechanism and instrument of the mind, but so close to it, so apt to its use that it will truly be an extension of humans.

Man will no longer need documentation to become an omniscient being like God himself. A less ultimate degree will create instrumentation acting across any distance which simultaneously combines radio broadcasts, x-rays, cinema and microscopic photography.

All the things in the universe and all those of man will be registered remotely as they are produced. Thus the reflected image of the world will be established - the world's complete memory, its true duplicate.

Anyone will be able to consult information remotely from afar, expanded or limited to the desired subject, projected on their individual screen.

Thus, in their armchair at home or in their place of work, anyone will be able to contemplate the whole of creation, or any part of it."

Many in the audience have heard Paul deliver these words before. Some appreciate the implications of these words, others do not. Sitting next to Paul's wife Cato is Henri La Fontaine. He carries a neatly folded copy of the speech Paul delivers on the occasion of Henri's 80th birthday celebration exactly one month ago. These are the words of that speech, and they sum up almost everything in Paul's heart.

"Henri La Fontaine! I met him in 1892 and here we are in 1934. That's forty-two years! But that is only a split-second! In the course of which the Mundaneum was conceived, created, developed, defended, modified, expanded, saved and replanted. In those distant times, La Fontaine was a mysterious person to the common man. Because, while he was very much a barrister, like me, and while he enjoyed independent means, like me, and while he was quite indifferent about what was said about him, yes, like me, he was also a pacifist and a feminist, which I most definitely was not.

We were both enamoured by internationalism – an alias for what we later called "mondiality," a new word that was very much barbaric to the French ears of our friends. We were practical idealists following different routes, and we had come to realize that nothing was possible without Documentation, a word we coined ourselves.

We set up our International Office of Bibliography in the Hotel Ravenstein, in premises no greater than 5 square metres, along with our little annexe in an old building that had belonged to the Lords of that same name, hidden away in the maze of a quarter of the city that is now demolished. As our yellowing photographs show, the first International Conference of Bibliography in 1895 founded our Institute. When La Fontaine and I meet up with each other now, seeming hardly to have changed at all except for a little whitening of the hair and stooping of the shoulders, we do so at the World Palace, yes Palace, to deal with the business of the Union of International Associations which, together, we summoned into existence in 1910.

We have always been companions in travel and intellectual adventure, always free from the shackles of the official world, always striving toward greater cooperation.

Certainly Henri La Fontaine never hung back from work. He is a being made from steel, with the eyes of a twenty-year old, for whom ten or eleven hours of work in a day is quite natural. Bibliographic work was a form of diversion while he went about winning the Nobel prize, went to meetings for socialist workers, tinkled at the piano, presided over the Senate, or officialised in Geneva as the Belgian delegate to The League of Nations.

Was our work at the Mundaneum only a diversion or were these other functions incidental? Only Madame La Fontaine can say. She tells the story of her honeymoon spent in correcting card-index proofs. She was present at the attack of acute "decimalitis" which gripped her husband for years. What a lot of battles for a pacifist like him, who, persuaded of the justice and usefulness of causes, let himself easily be led by this combatant who toiled at his side to gain ever new conquests of intellectual organisation!

I think of those who have toiled for us for thirty years, especially those indispensable women Poels and de Bauche, and those of our blessed printers, Lamberty and Van Keerberghen, who have been as keen as us to avoid typographical errors and to deliver on time.

Yesterday, we assembled to discuss the heart-breaking decision of the Minister of Public Works who told us - Off you go then! All our quarters, a hundred rooms, a hectare chock full of data to be evacuated within forty five days. Ah! This innocent executioner of a Minister! He is truly sapping us just when so much remains to be done. He lacks documentation, this cruel man. Because he does not want the inconvenience of coming to see for himself, he, who is responsible for our buildings, he is unaware that there are files containing deeds that assert our legal and moral rights in the registries of his colleagues for Sciences, Arts, Justice, even Foreign Affairs.

Once again Henri La Fontaine's name has been linked with Paul Otlet's. Today, in the same mocking tones as ten years ago, twenty years ago, forty years ago, we are the "enlightened ones" who have filled the Great Hall of the Mundeaneum with cards covered with cabalistic decimal signs, preventing its use for more practical and lucrative purposes, we have been exposed to public condemnation.

Ah! My dear Henri, when our glances met during this verdict, didn't they reveal a lofty melancholy that automatically caused us to shrug our shoulders? Together we have seen so much of this kind of thing, and surely so much has tumbled down around us in these last few decades that we are filled with an ironic indulgence for these people who truly "know not what they do."

You were more resigned than I was when I said we had to explain to our opponent what he had done. But we are as fervent as one another when we conclude that, tomorrow like yesterday, long may our Mundaneum our beloved Institute live!"

Henri La Fontaine, 1934

Paul Otlet, 1934

Chapter 14

October 1934
Mundaneum, Palais Mondial, Brussels, Belgium

As all funds finally run out for the Mundaneum in the Autumn of 1934, Paul does what he does best. He publishes a masterpiece of ambition. It is so far ahead of its time, that outside of Paul's immediate circle only the likes of the science fiction visionary HG Wells seem able to fully appreciate it. Although history sometimes declares it to be Paul's definitive publication, history is yet to happen, and when he offers his 500 page *Traité de Documentation* to the world, the world takes little notice. Paul's book is not translated into English or any other language except Russian, and it is not until the arrival of artificial intelligence several generations later that a bad English translation eventually appears. Even now, there is not a fully readable copy of the book online in any language except French.

The reason that the original manuscript gets to the printers at all is not due to the mind of Paul Otlet but to the labours of a teenage *au pair* called Wilhelmina Coops. She is the younger sister of one of Paul's data processors at the Mundaneum, and the turn of events is best set out in her own words. Here is what she says, translated from her original French.

"When I arrived in Brussels in the autumn, I was still very young. I thought that as an au-pair for the Otlets I would be helping out in the house, but instead I ended up working with the professor himself on finishing his book. When I first met him, the writing of the book was mostly done, but his handwriting was so difficult to decipher that the printer had a really hard time working with the manuscript. So it became my job to correct the typeset proofs, but often there were words that neither the printer nor I could decipher, and we had to go back and keep asking. But the professor often had no time for us. So it was down to me to make the text as understandable as possible. I think I did a good job."

There is also evidence that the young woman and the old man build a close relationship during their months together. On the title page of the final proofs from the printer, Paul writes the following note of thanks to Wilhelmina, "After five months of work together behind the same table, here it is. Now it is our turn to sow the good seed of documentation, of institution, and of the Mundaneum."

But surprising evidence of the way the girl treats the great man is to be found many years later, discovered in a margarine box, between dozens of notes, tickets, postcards and letters, all folded to the size of an index card. The card is reproduced in this book, and it reads as follows.

"Paul, leave me the key to the house, because I forgot mine. Just put it on your desk in the small index card box."

The full English title of Paul Otlet's most important work is tortuous, *A Treatise on Documentation, the Book on the Book, Theory and Practice*, but it not only predicts the arrival of the world wide web, search engines, tabs, desktop work stations, hyperlinks, and everything else familiar to the online children of today, it also proposes a methodology of how to construct them.

Paul is the child of both a blessed and a cursed generation. The curse of his generation is of a world at war, but the blessing of his generation is of a world of new technological wonders. All of his contemporaries suffer from the same curse and similarly they all enjoy the same blessings, but Paul is unique in being first to recognise how such new technological wonders can be harnessed and combined to function together in order to defeat the curse of war. Let us count these blessings.

In the 1870s the telephone, the phonograph and the

typewriter all begin to make an impact. The Burroughs calculating machine is patented in 1885. In the 1890s the Hollerith voting machine uses punch cards to record and store political data, and the player piano uses the same binary punch-holes to program, store and retrieve data for musical entertainment. Radio rises to dominance in the early 1920s and lately the television arrives in 1925.

In this book *Traité de Documentation*, Paul includes the full specification for a circular workstation, a smart desk for multiple projects to be switched as they rotate. He clearly describes the advantages of this concept in a way that anyone can understand who is familiar with the multiple windows and tabs of contemporary computer interfaces. This concept is literally revolutionary, it is shaped like a revolving spoked wheel. But Paul's vision is almost limitless. He takes on board the availability of the telephone, phonograph audio recording, the typewriter, calculating machine, punch card, radio, television and "as yet many inventions to be discovered," including the reading and editing of remote documents, artificially-generated speech and "electric telescopes". This is in 1934, which may seem prescient, but Paul has already been expounding these notions for decades!

He discusses the need for text to be stored in a form that can be searched, located, analysed and edited, then automatically reformatted and shared with anyone, anywhere, at will, and all at the touch of a button or the spin of the wheel or the flick of a lever.

He needs to invent new terminology such as a "monographic principle" for handling text, "deep indexing" for handling information and "hyper documentation" for manipulating text. He even speculates about what happens to data links when the content of a bit of information is freed from its original boundaries and repurposed for something else. In a parallel with atomic theory and the implications of splitting atoms, he wonders how all this can be controlled so that the results are beneficial to the individual and to society in general, rather than an artificial intelligence that get out of control and cause more harm than good.

Of course Paul has already cracked the problem of mass data storage and retrieval in the *Mundaneum*, albeit using a combination of available technology in the form of smart indexing and smart women. Now he proposes using programmable punch cards not only to sort and retrieve items of information, but also to handle all the individual little chunks that make up that item of information.

Next he turns his mind to how he can make everything work to the advantage of a future society using new technology, and his mind is never less than astonishing. Paul not only brings his previous theories up to date, but he proposes completely new forms of electrical printing, with machines for making photocopies including pocket-sized personal copiers. Certain academics in 1934 would by now regard his book as the fantasies of a dreamer at best and the ravings of a lunatic at worst, but Paul shows no mercy, and goes on to force-feed his audience the concept of computer-aided-design. What if, he speculates, what if illustrations, graphics and charts can be created from a library of basic units of design. What if these graphic components can be called up, manipulated and reassembled any which way.

He integrates his long-held belief that machines are needed to translate the human voice to machine writing and vice versa. He names one a *telereading* machine to allow text to be read from a network of terminals, with a *telescription* machine to allow the transmission of edited and updated texts stored remotely, all without having to physically disturb the originals. He believes it is possible for users to read remotely-stored documents on their screens at home. These home screens can be linked by wires just like telephones, or they can be wireless like radios or new-fangled televisions. Homes and workplaces need not be restricted to a single screen, but can have multiple screens which can be made smart using microphones and loudspeakers to call up documents and play multimedia. Frequently used functions can be left open on their screen for instant access, and others can be open and shut as needed, like doors and windows in a wall.

Can the reader surrender yet? In a word, No! Paul goes on to demonstrate how a completely new work environment will exist for factories, offices and home-workers, and eventually all of the machinery he describes can be brought together, coordinated, fused into a single unit and then miniaturised.

In 1899's *The Sleeper* Awakes, 1907's *The War in the Air*, and 1914's *The World Set Free*, the English novelist and futurist HG Wells predicts cryogenics, the video-disc and the atomic bomb. But he makes sure that his readers are anchored in the real world in which he sets the action. Paul does much the same, and is careful not to introduce technology that is beyond the imagination. For example, in the *Traité* he includes the design for a mobile filing cabinet the size of coffin mounted on a circular rail, which looks highly comical. Then he goes on to regurgitate his old work concerning the benefits of microfilm for data storage, which succeeds in negating the need for his filing cabinet on rails in the first place. These occasional slips are forgivable, but Paul's astoundingly ambitious book attracts a depressingly limited readership.

Some say that Paul Otlet rips off the hugely popular writings of HG Wells in describing a data resource that Paul calls the *Encyclopedia Microphotica Mundaneum*, with Wells setting out in his concept of a "world encyclopedia" in his own masterwork *The Work, Wealth and Happiness of Mankind* which is published three years before Paul's book in 1931. Those who say so speak from ignorance, because Otlet sketches out the first draft of these concepts way back in 1891. It is much more likely that HG Wells takes inspiration from none other than his fellow internationalist and pacifist Henri La Fontaine, and it is certain that those two men meet several times at peace conferences and awards ceremonies, where they discuss Paul's concepts and innovations.

There are many remarkable diagrams and illustrations in Paul's *Traité de Documentation*, but there is one pair of hand-drawn sketches that are probably as pivotal as the entire treatise. On two sheets of paper, catalogued as Documents 8440 and 8441 by P. Otlet for the *Encyclopedia Universalis Mundaneum* and headed *Documentation et Telecommunication*, there is a series of frames set out like a graphic novel with captions in childish capital letters.

Frame 1 shows a matrix of mixed media combining telephones, radios, audio discs, film and television, and how these are combined to allow live conference calls.

Frame 2 shows a number of subscribers in remote locations, each wearing a set of headphones and each connected to a telephone terminal. Their telephones are linked to a central data hub. The caption reads, "National or international committee meeting. Subscribers can listen and speak and are connected to one another through a hub at the central office."

The caption for Frame 3 reads, "Congress Session, held in the presence of members who are on remote sites." The illustration is of a large number of users in Brussels seated in front of a wide-screen presentation linked by hard wire and wirelessly. The split-screen shows the same image as the one shown in Brussels being viewed by remote groups of subscribers in distant locations including Paris.

In Frame 4 there is a device sitting on a desk. The device looks exactly like a modern flat-screen with a letterbox aspect ratio. It is wireless and it is shown scanning a document. There is a television connected to the device which displays the identical image of the scanned document. The caption reads, "Transmission of document graphics by television screen."

Frame 5 expands the range of media, and shows more than one scanner linked to telephones and televisions and delivering audio from disc and images from film of a recorded video. The accompanying text says, "Stored data (on disc or film) sent by telephone or television."

Frame 6 occupies the whole width of the page, and is heavily annotated. Top-left is a series of catalogued data labelled books, films, audio discs and "objects". Next is the entire content of the Mundaneum miniaturised to fit on two tables and mechanically linked to a series of scanners. The extracted data is then transmitted through a screening unit and delivered to remote television screens. Paul's hand-written annotations are too long to fit in the panel and get squashed into the bottom of the space, showing the speed at which he is working. They read as follows.

"(A) Documentation consisting of collections and catalogs will duplicate the entire content of the *Mundaneum*.

(B and C) Here, machines will help with complementary operations, analysis and synthesis, needed to deliver whatever encyclopedic knowledge the user demands.

(D) The requested elements will be mechanically extracted.

(E) Transmitters will launch them into the universal network from where they will be received by workstations."

These two pages, Document 8440 and Document 8441, are enough justification for half the strapline of this book, "The Man Who Invented The Internet." The final illustration on page 450 of the volume reveals how Paul really feels about the government's treatment of him, and it is worthy of his father the Egomaniac.

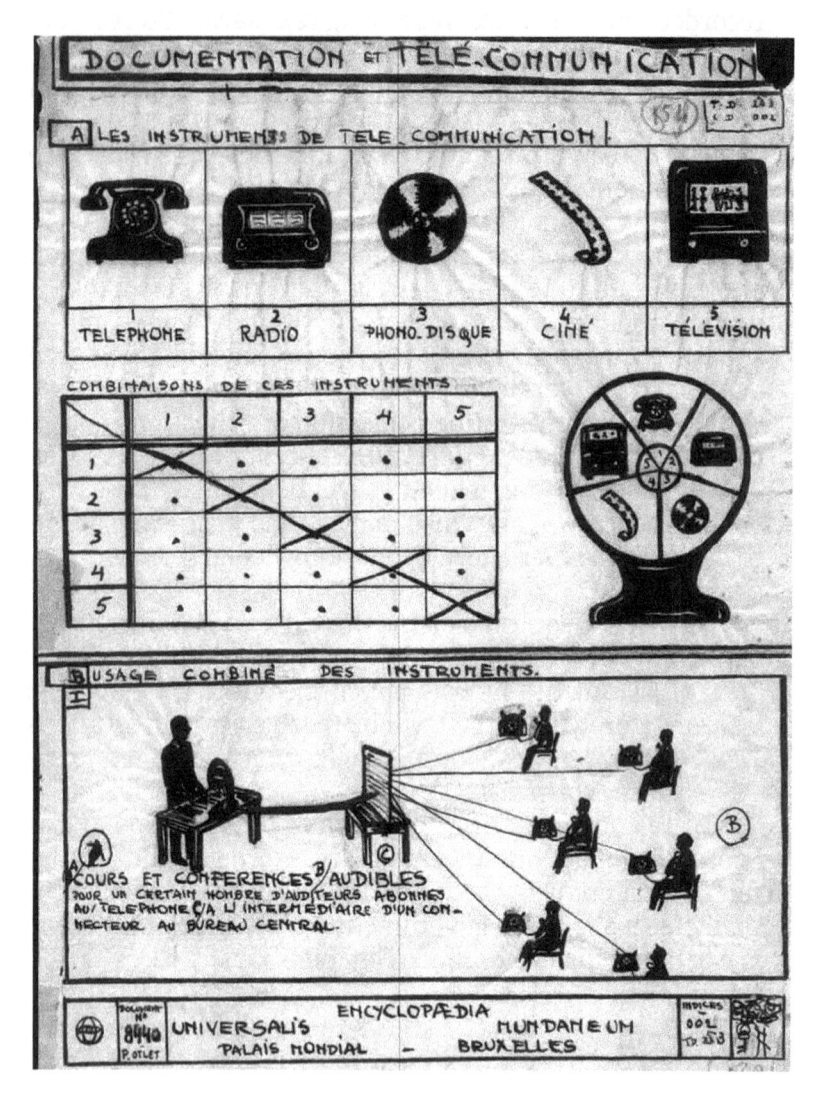

Document 8440, sketch design for the internet, 1934, Paul Otlet

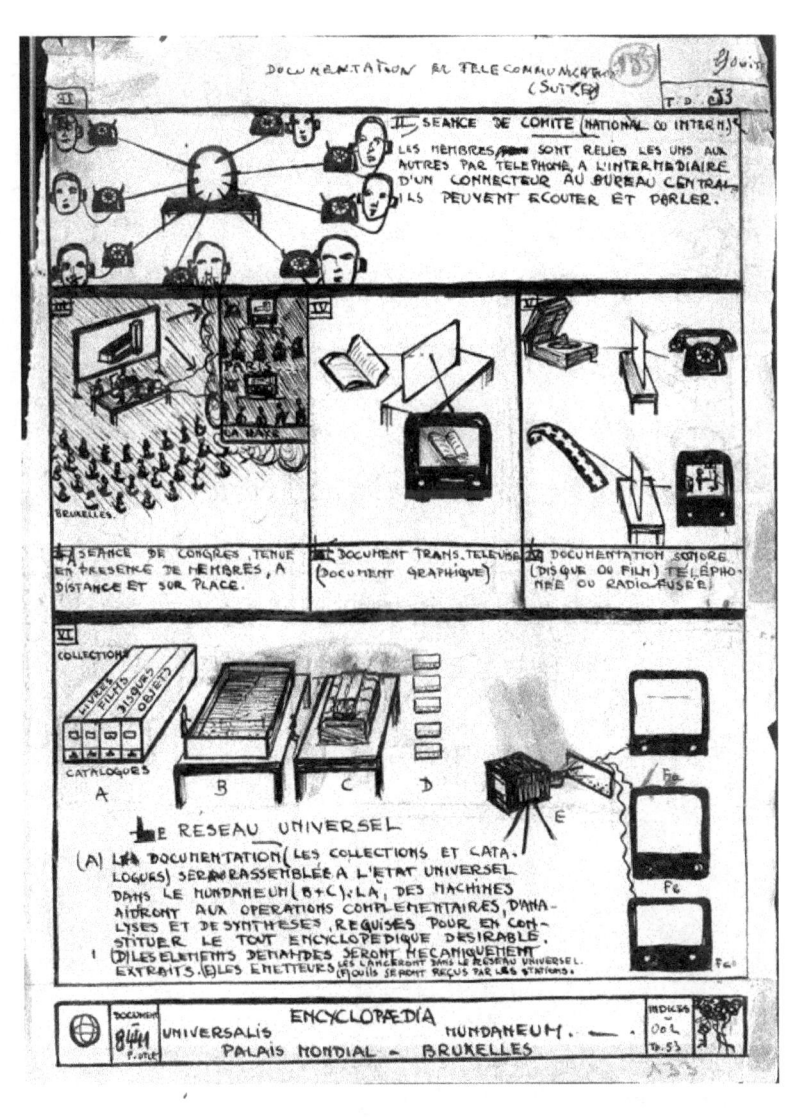

*Document 8441, sketch design for the internet,
1934, Paul Otlet*

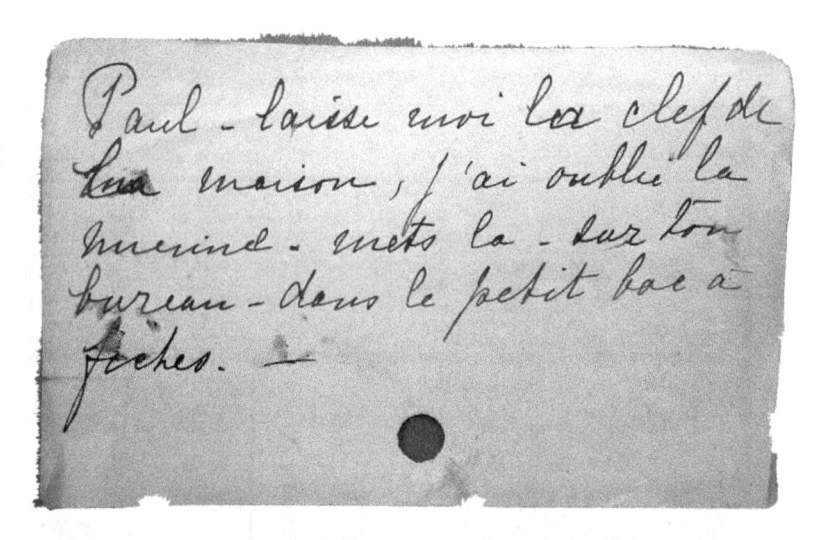

The private note from Wilhelmina Coops to Paul Otlet, 1934

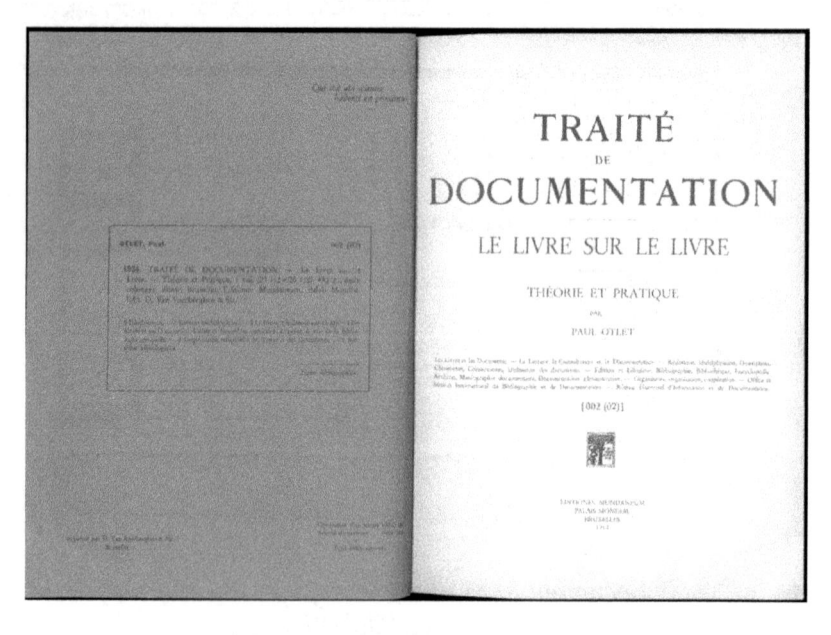

Traité de Documentation title page, 1934

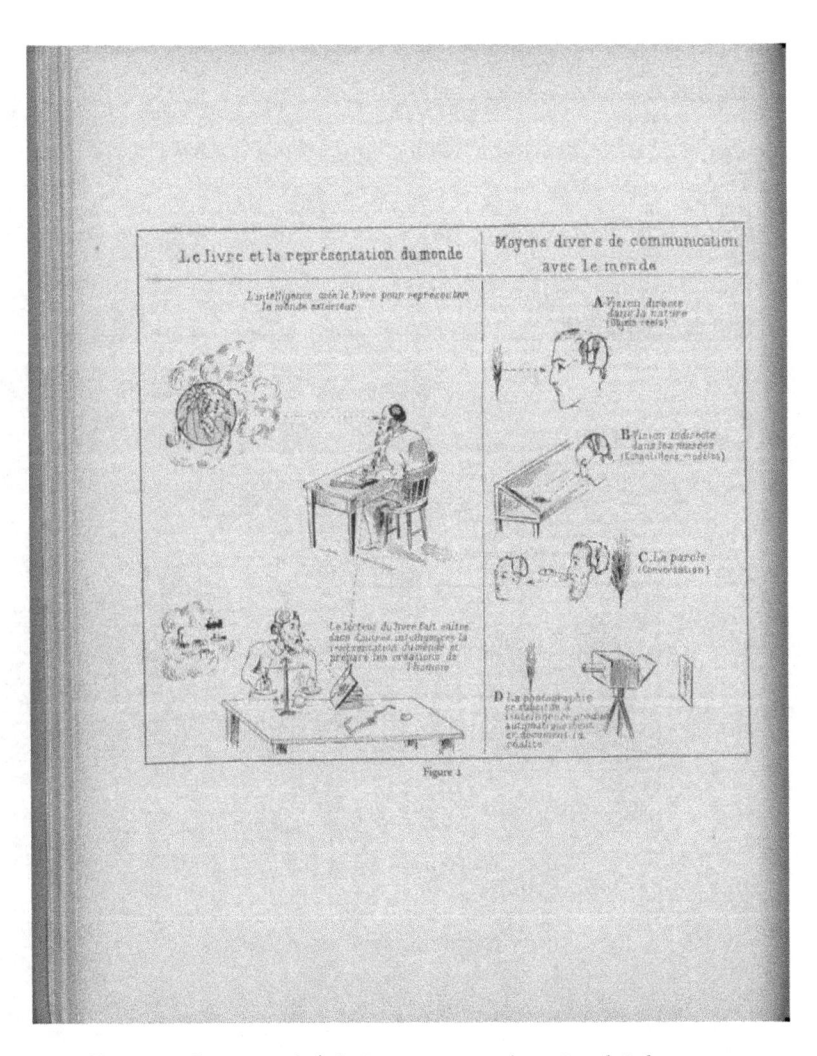

diagram from Traité de Documentation, Paul Otlet 1934

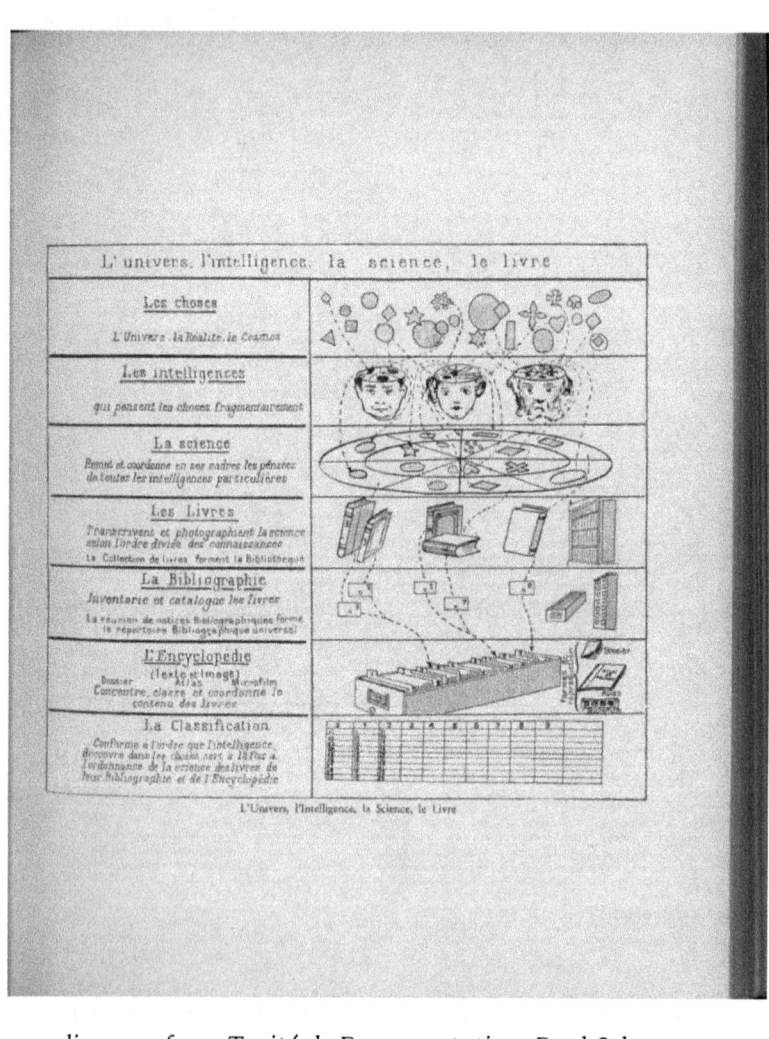

diagram from Traité de Documentation, Paul Otlet 1934

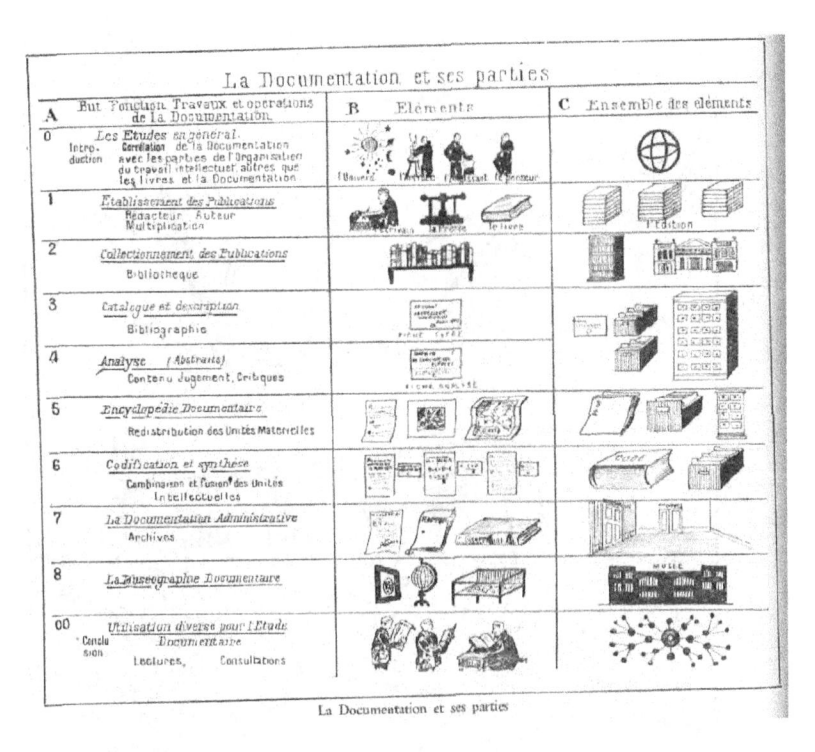

diagram from Traité de Documentation, *Paul Otlet 1934*

Page 450 of Traité de Documentation, by Paul Otlet, 1934.

Chapter 15

23 August 1938
Rue de Florence 13, Brussels

  The Mundaneum remains closed, its massive archive is left to gather dust and rot, a life's work abandoned. Today is Paul's seventieth birthday. Perhaps it is inevitable that he has become introspective and melancholy and that he now reviews his life not with a sense of satisfaction but with so many regrets. He believes he can remember back to when he was a little boy being taken to a photographer's studio for his birthday image to be captured. That was some years after his mother died. He thinks he can remember a studio filled with wooden drawers for reference cards and photographic plates. He certainly remembers the shock of moving to Paris and the librarian at school who seems so fierce at first but then turns out to be so kind to him, and helps to reveal Dewey's index system for the first time. And he remembers where it is all applied for the first time in that little room next to the Staircase of the Jews. A life's work indeed, but what was it all for?
  There is one constant thing in the long life of Paul Otlet, more constant that Henri La Fontaine, more constant than his wife Cato, more constant than the Mundaneum itself, and that continuum is made up of his own diaries, which he has kept meticulously since he was that child at the photographer's. Paul finds himself drawn to the cabinet where his diaries are kept, wondering if they really are all that's left. At least Henri La Fontaine has a grand piano for company, and he plays with it like a maestro. And to think, Henri is almost eighty-four.
  Paul believes he has done everything he can to ensure his work with La Fontaine continues, but he knows in all honesty that he has become isolated and difficult to work

with since the cash ran out. As for his wife, who stands by him no matter what, even her patience is not inexhaustible. Now he can't support her, in fact it is her inheritance that supports him, and the most recent pages of his diary confirm that he feels like a gigolo.

"Cato, my dear wife, has been absolutely devoted to my work. All her savings and even her jewels testify to that. The way I invade her house testifies to it. Her collaboration testifies to it. Her wish to see everything finished after I'm dead and gone testifies to it. Her modest little fortune has saved my work and my mind. But I have not."

The fact that Hitler is in Vienna compounds Paul's misery even more. Only a fool can believe that another European war is avoidable, and the former-celebrity Paul Otlet is certainly no fool. Perhaps he has been foolish to believe that the government would honour their promise to fund him for reopening the Mundaneum, but he knows on this day of all days that the dream is over. He turns the page of his diary and begins to write more.

"Such a long life, and what have I done with it? Cato has opened my eyes to the truth. The Mundaneum will never be restored. It was she who dealt with Le Corbusier and his plans for the World City, and it is she who assures me that glorious project will never be built either. I make Cato suffer, even though she has been the only person who has really loved me, and proved it continuously. But I cannot ask her to exceed the limits of her good will.

I have imposed an unbearable life on her for far too long. She has had nothing to look forward to except my failure. She has suffered too much. And I know that she has become indifferent to my work. Can I demand that we go on like this? The answer is No! I do not want her to suffer and I don't want to make my work suffer. So I must choose between my two loves and my two duties, and I know I can't unite them.

I must choose Cato, because she is the living reality

and she represents the highest level of humanity to me. I now see my work as an abstraction. Only an abstraction."

There is another reason why Paul must choose Cato over his dreams for the Mundaneum, and the reason is that she gives him an ultimation. Essentially it's a simple choice between his Mundaneum or his wife. At their age she cannot go on supporting his failure, or bolster unrealistic hopes for a miracle to recreate his world-wide network of knowledge and information. Simply put, she can't take it any more and has had enough.

And so it is that Paul Otlet and a few loyal helpers try to rescue what they can to put the Mundaneum's mechanics and data in some sort of order, but there is no longer any drive or heart in the project. He is careful not to risk his duties to Cato, and retreats behind his old desk in his old study. How Cato feels is unknown. If she keeps a diary herself, or expresses her feelings in letters to friends and family, they remain private.

Henri La Fontaine retreats behind his grand piano. He too knows that another war is coming, and that it will be a total disaster for all his plans of a federation of nations united in peace and prosperity. He also knows that he cannot have that long to live, and he extracts a final promise from his old friend Paul Otlet. In March 1942, he holds Paul to that promise.

Paul Otlet, centre, at the former Palais Mondial archway

Paul and Cato Otlet, left, with the last of the Mundaneum team

above and below, the abandoned Mundaneum

Henri La Fontaine after the final closure of the Mundaneum

surviving files from the original Mundaneum

PART TWO

HANS HAGEMEYER

THE MAN WHO DESTROYED THE INTERNET

Chapter 16

September 1907
Brinkmannstrasse boys school, Hemelingen, Germany

Little Johann is not happy as a rule, but on this special day he is not even happy with his own name. In fact he refuses to answer to his name at all and insists that now he is all grown up he wants to be called by his mother's name for him, which is Hans. He raises his *schultüte* as if it is a flaming torch and not the traditional paper cone given to all German boys on their first day at big school. The paper cornucopia is filled with bribes to sweeten the shock that his new school and the new regime is about to inflict on him. He has his own coping mechanism for dealing with shock, and the way that he copes is to distract himself by compiling lists.

In the celebration paper cone there are four pencils, an exercise book, a ruler, a fistful of chestnuts, a five-pfennig bar of chocolate, a wooden soldier and all sorts of other stuff and nonsense. "Hans" sits in a corner of the classroom and carefully unpacks everything so that the items are laid out in a symmetrical pattern. Then he takes the notebook, the pencil and the ruler to make a neat list of all the other items in his *schultüte*. Once his own list is finished, he asks other boys to spread out their own gifts so that he can make lists of those things too. Hans likes making lists. It is a habit since he first learns to write. It comforts him and makes him feel less unhappy.

The school is newly-built and very modern. To Hans it seems huge and somewhat daunting, but it is nothing that he cannot take in his little stride. The school is a long way from home, in fact it is more than twenty minutes walk away, near the right bank of the river Weser. There are seven classes with over fifty boys in each one. There is a portrait of Kaiser Wilhelm on the wall of each class. Hans thinks the Kaiser looks silly with that eagle-shaped moustache pointing up to his eyebrows and a skull-and-crossbones hussar busby perched on top of his head. Hans can confuse portraits of the Kaiser with pictures of King Edward and Tsar Nicholas. They look almost the same as one another, apart from the cut of their facial hair. And there is something else that confuses the boy. They all used to be friends, but now the King and the Tsar don't want to be friends with the Kaiser any more. Hans tries to understand this, and wonders if it is because the three rulers are cousins, because sometimes his own cousins can be nice but at other times they can be really, really horrible.

The teachers at his new school live in their own quarters away at the back, out of earshot from the noise of the day boys. They emerge from their lairs to force-feed Hans twelve hours of reading a week, as well as six hours of religion, five hours of arithmetic and three hours of singing sturdy anthems and patriotic songs. He does not enjoy his religious lessons very much. He finds them repetitive and boring. He does not mind the singing though, and some of the more rousing songs make him tingle in quite a pleasant way. The arithmetic lessons are easy, and Hans is ahead of most of the other boys when it comes to memorising multiplication tables and doing sums in his head. But it is books that he likes the best, particularly when he is allowed access to the library. Hans likes the library very much.

The library occupies the top floor of the four-storey school, which is a plain white Art Deco structure that looks more like a geometrical factory building than a centre of education. In a way it is a factory, a factory for the manufacture of model German males. And like the latest factory buildings, the library has a row of metal-framed windows running all the way along one side. Hans is unfamiliar with the operation of modern metal windows, and he especially likes the rods and levers that operate them for light and ventilation. When nobody is looking, he goes along the entire wall and adjusts every window so that it is at exactly the same angle as its neighbour. As well as lists, Hans also likes symmetry.

The only library he is familiar with before coming to this new school is an old dark and dusty interior in the middle of Bremen, where he sometimes accompanies his father on a mysterious mission to do with the family business. He doesn't really understand what his father does, but it takes up a lot of time and involves a lot of talking. In the old Bremen library, boys are not even allowed to talk, let alone explore the shelves. But here at school Hans is able to find all sorts of information to help him organise his lists.

There is a wooden cabinet with sliding drawers full of index cards, and he works out how the numbers on the cards refer to the numbers written on the spines of all the books. He begins to make a list of reference numbers of the things that interest him, like railways and uniforms, and when he finds a book that is not in its correct order, he gains great satisfaction from moving it to where he thinks it should be. The books themselves are too difficult to read for an eight-year-old, but their indexing is easy.

Hans is regarded by the other boys as a loner, but he is not bullied or left out of communal activities. As for the teachers, they show no special interest in him whatsoever. He may not be happy, but he finds sanctuary in the library and therapy in his list-making, and he soon discovers that this is about as good as it gets.

the first day at the new school, 1907

*Kaiser Wilhelm II
classroom portrait in Death's-head Hussar uniform*

Chapter 17

November 1923
University of Jena, Free State of Thuringia, Germany

Hans is not a happy young man. For almost three years before going to university he labours out in the fields. Back then, he wants to fight in Flanders but the authorities disqualify him because he is underage. He knows more about muck and bullets than any of the pansies or Semites who try to teach him here at the university, and now they have the audacity to appoint a new professor to take charge of his course who isn't even a man. Her name is Margarete von Wrangell. Which is feminism under the guise of science. And the Wrangell woman isn't even German, she is dragged up in Moscow. Whatever next? Women judges from Eskimoland, female doctors from Africa!

A hand-written pamphlet appears on the faculty notice board, denouncing this von Wrangell as a betrayer of the traditional role of German women in society, *Kinder, Küche, Kirche* – children, kitchen, church. Hans agrees with the sentiment, but is unhappy with the fact that the poster is badly written and much too generic. He believes that what will rouse both students and staff against Margarete von Wrangell is a spot of character assassination, and if the facts don't fit then they can be invented. He would write such a pamphlet himself, but he cannot be bothered.

Hans is not a happy young man. Not happy at all. In fact he's completely had it with university. Yesterday's mass demonstration and speeches by students achieve nothing. Placards and chants never do, because everybody knows that actions speak louder than words.

Germany is well and truly finished, and so is this sclerotic university. Not content with appointing women to join the homos and Jews, the idiot governors have even banned duelling, so how does a man have some innocent fun any more? Stuff this place, and stuff these so-called studies. He can slink off back home and work for his father, who admittedly is a bit of a stickler but his heart's in the right place. That's if the Reds haven't taken over, and his father still has a business. Although why the Reds would want to take over the dump that is Hemelingen is beyond him. Who knows what the future holds?

In the case of Hans Hagemeyer the future dictates that he lives to the ripe old age of 94, and in October 1993 he dies an old age pensioner in his Saxon bed. But as for now, the young Hans rises from his brass-studded chair in this magnificent library for the last time. The walls are lined with tens of thousands of books, maybe hundreds of thousands. He could never navigate the stupid indexing system to find anything of use to him. He has forgotten more about the theories of agriculture than he has ever learned here. He pulls out his student cap with its cowardly white stripe above the peak and throws it away, then he heads South to the corner along *Oberlauengasse* towards *Zur Noll* for a beer, maybe two. It depends on what beer costs today. At the beginning of term a glass of beer cost 250 Reichsmarks. Yesterday it was 200 billion. What is a billion anyway?

It's all the fault of the Belgians. Just because Germany refuses to pay for outrageous reparations, in gold for God's sake, the Walloons walk into the Ruhr valley without a shot being fired and start commandeering our factories. That's why our workers are on strike. That's why the idiots in Berlin are running out of rags and paper to print more money. It's all the fault of the Belgians.

Today the beer is still 200 billion a half litre. The landlord is probably short of time to check the newspaper and put up the price. Hans removes the local paper from its wooden frame and slops his glass to a table near the door. A pile of horseshit is stacked up outside.

The paper is full of a riot in a Munich beer hall, led by good old Ludendorff. Now there's a man who knows who's who and what's what when it comes to the conspiracy that's allowed the Belgians in. And it is not just the Semites and the Reds, but the Freemasons too. Good God! The paper reveals all. A horde of members of Ludendorff's party battling it out with the cops, and a dozen of them killed. The old warhorse looks calm as you like in the black dots that make up the newspaper picture. And right next to him, looking like Charlie Chaplin sucking a lemon, little Adolf Hitler. Ludendorff needs to dump him pronto. That Hitler is a clown.

Margarete von Wrangell, first German woman professor

*Ludendorff and Hitler,
leaders of the beer hall riot, 1923*

20 billion Reichsmark note, 1923

Chapter 18

December 1924
Landsberg Prison, Bavaria, Germany

In Belgium, Paul Otlet officially renames his *Palais Mondial* the Mundaneum, and begins work on his insanely grand project for a *Cité Mondiale*. Simultaneously in Germany, Adolf Hitler is released from jail after serving nine months of a five year sentence for treason. While he is in prison, scheming and seething, Hitler begins work on an insanely grand project for *Germania*, a global city to act as the centre for ceremony, order and world domination.

Germania is Hitler's plan for the renewal of Berlin. A megacity to be constructed as the core of a Thousand Year Reich. A new word capital for a new world empire. A scheme so lunatic in its scale that it needs a lunatic of Hitler's calibre to drive it forward. Adolf sketches out his ideas for a megacity in *Mein Kampf*, the autobiographical manifesto he writes while in prison, and he accompanies it with illustrations for massive monuments and streetscapes. Later he ropes in an ambitious architect called Albert Speer, who he appoints General Building Inspector of the Reich and tasks him with bringing the vision of *Germania* to life.

His vision is applauded by the movers and shakers in the Nazi party, including a rising star named Alfred Rosenberg. *Mein Kampf* is where Hans Hagemeyer first encounters an ideology that seems to chime with his own discontent, and as a young man in a dead-end job the vision of *Germania* is inspiring to him.

In due course, whole districts of his capital city get erased to make way for the planned megalopolis, with dispossessed Berliners rehoused in properties seized from Jewish families. Giant projects are incorporated into the overall plan, including the Olympic Stadium, the

Chancellery, the International Convention Centre and Tempelhof Airport. Huge boulevards are planned, ideal for military parades. And of course there is to be a gigantic palace for none other than Adolf Hitler himself.

At one end of the main city axis, a triumphal arch is planned, inscribed with the names of 1,800,000 dead German soldiers of the Great War, transforming the 1918 defeat into victory. Hitler declares, "In the shortest possible time, Berlin must be redeveloped and acquire the form that reflects the greatness of our victory as the capital of a powerful new empire. In the completion of what is now our country's most important architectural task, I see it as the most significant contribution to our final victory, and I expect it to be completed by the year 1950."

The crowning glory of *Germania* is to be a gigantic monumental domed People's Hall, designed by architect Albert Speer with the sole purpose of worshiping the Nazi doctrines in general and the Führer in particular. One day Speer confirms this in an interview, saying "Hitler believed that as centuries passed, his huge domed assembly hall would acquire great holy significance and become a hallowed shrine as important to National Socialism as Saint Peters in Rome is to Catholicism. Cultism was at the root of the entire plan."

Unfortunately, Adolf is not an engineer, and he fails to appreciate that the city of Berlin is built on a bog which cannot possibly hold the weight of his dreams, but Albert Speer does not dare tell him because Adolf Hitler is confirmed by most historians as being divorced from reality. Nonetheless, Hans Hagemeyer sees Berlin as a city of opportunity, and begins to dream that he is destined to live there one day.

Germania city concept, Adolf Hitler and Albert Speer

Germania planners Albert Speer and Adolf Hitler

Chapter 19

October 31st 1929
Bremen, Germany

The pagan rituals of Hallowe'en are widely celebrated in the United States of America, but have yet to take hold in Germany. A hollowed pumpkin-head lantern flickers in the darkened doorway of the American Consular Agency. Inside the dull rhombus of the building on this All Souls Night the atmosphere is distinctly bizarre. A telegraph chatters behind double doors and a group of middle-aged men huddle round the message tape trying to absorb the stream of news. Their faces are grim, they are in deep shock, but there is nothing to say. The Wall Street Crash of two days ago is now in economic freefall with fourteen billion dollars of investment wiped out. Offers of sale of some of their stocks attract no buyers at any price whatsoever.

Every man in the room is affected, some badly, some completely. Along with all other foreign capitalists, these men withdraw their stakes in their German investments and the economy of Germany begins to crumble. In another two weeks it collapses entirely, taking the government with it and leaving a power vacuum.

Deeper in the city, Hans sits alone in front of a small coal fire. He is armed against the crisis with nothing but a commercial apprenticeship, working as an authorised signatory for his father's company in his birth city of Bremen, with investments in the city's new intercontinental shipping terminus. Since July, the service between Bremen and New York offers a weekly voyage for two thousand passengers to cross the Atlantic aboard the luxury liner named *SS Bremen* after its home city. It is financed by the delegation in the American Consular Agency who face disaster. As of now, there is no work for Hans to do, and no money to pay him for the work already done. He is not a happy man.

There is a pompous fellow who also works in his father's company and this pompous fellow suggests that Hans could cling on to some sort of economic advantage if he joins the local Freemason's lodge. Hans knows next to nothing of Freemasonry other than the accusations that they are part of the conspiracy responsible for helping cause the current economic fiasco. The pompous fellow is not insistent, but he palms Hans a battered booklet. It looks ancient, and it smells of the old library his father used to take him to when he was a boy. On the cover there is a Masonic icon of a draftsman's set-square topped by compass dividers. Inside the cover is a weird illustration of masonic figure with arms arranged like a swastika.

Hans pokes the fire, which flickers like the pumpkin-head lantern. He opens the booklet at a random page and begins to read the nonsense printed there.

"In the presence of The Grand Architect Of The Universe, and of this worthy, worshipful and warranted Lodge of Ancient Free and Accepted Masons, regularly assembled and properly dedicated, of my own free will and accord, I do hereby and hereon solemnly swear that I will always heed, conceal and never reveal any part of the secrets and mysteries of Free and Accepted Masons in Masonry, unless it be to a true and lawful Brother or Brethren.

The Worshipful Master presses the fingers of his left hand on The Candidate's right hand, then presses the fingers of his left hand on the Volume Of Sacred Law.

I likewise solemnly swear that I will not write these secrets, indite, carve, mark, engrave, or otherwise delineate them, or cause or suffer it to be done by others if in my power to prevent it, on anything, movable or immovable under the canopy of Heaven, whereby or whereon, any letter, character, or figure, or the least trace of any letter, character, or figure, may become legible or intelligible to myself or to anyone in the world, lest our secret art and hidden mysteries may improperly become known through my unworthiness.

The Worshipful Master touches the Candidate's right hand again, the Deacons lower their wands and all make the Sign of Freemasonary. The Junior Warden unties the knot of the hoodwink. The Worshipful Master raises his gavel on high and points it right, left, right again, and coinciding with the removal of the hoodwink, sounds the gavel, at which moment the Brethren clap their hands as the Junior Warden takes the head of the Candidate to direct his gaze ..."

The candle inside the pumpkin-head lantern gutters, smokes and burns out, as Hans sighs, spits into the fire, mutters a short expletive and carefully places the pamphlet on the coals. He watches as the cover turns one shade and then two shades of brown, and as the smoke begins to rise he sniffs it. After a while, he rummages in a desk drawer, pulls out a sheet of paper and a pencil, scratches his inner thigh and then begins to write a list. He still likes making lists, and this one will change his life.

launch of the luxury liner SS Bremen, 1929

illustration from Handbook of Freemasonary

Chapter 20

January 1931
Freikorps Headquarters, Oldenburg, Germany.

"Name?"
"Hagemeyer, Hans Johann Gerhard, *mein Standartenführer*. I have been sent here by ..."
"Please do not speak until spoken to, Herr Hagemeyer. What is your occupation?"
"I am a Librarian."
"Do you mean book-keeper?"
"No, *mein Standardrenführer*, my work is in the organisation of libraries."
"Organisation of libraries. So. You are an organiser. And what is your Address?"
"Oranienburger Strasse 79, Bremen."
"Place and date of birth?"
"Bremen, the thirtieth of March 1899."
"Marital status?"
"Married."
"Wife's name?"
"Erna"
"What is your father's name?'
"Hagemeyer, Hans Johann Friedrich. He is a well-respected businessman and ..."
"Please only answer the specific questions I put to you, Herr Hagemeyer. What is your father's place and date of birth?"
"Bremen, the third of March 1871."
"Give me the name of and your relationship to your NSDAP sponsor, and also give me his Party membership number."
"My sponsor is my employer, Otto Wagener, *mein Standartenführer*. His NSDAP Membership Number is

159,203. He is Chief of Staff of the *Sturmabteilung* and Founder of the party's Economic Press Office."

The uniformed man turns his back on Hans, in order to take a thick ledger from its shelf and search through the hand-written pages. The filing system is not what it should be, yet. There is an exaggerated pause.

"Thank you Herr Hagemeyer. Your membership status is approved. I congratulate you. Your Party membership number is 449,205. Sieg Heil!"

"Thank you, *mein Standartenführer*. Sieg Heil!"

At its peak, the NSDAP counts its membership at over eight and a half million, so for Hans to tuck in under the half million mark counts him as an early adopter. The *Sturmabteilung* is the paramilitary wing of the NSDAP or Nazi party, commonly known as storm troopers or brownshirts.

The party is lately rebranded from the German Workers Party to the National Socialist German Workers' Party, in order to appeal to both wings of current German ideals, with National aiming for the right and Socialist appealing to the left. Hans is in the former camp, but his real reason for joining the Party is not ideological. It is financial. In these days of mass unemployment there is good money to be made just for writing whatever propaganda the Party needs him to write, and he has a knack for doing exactly that. There is also another reason he is keen to join the ranks of the Nazis. He really likes the uniform.

At home, as he parades in his new finery in front of Erna his wife, she describes the uniform's light brown shades as cow-dung-by-moonlight, but she admits that the cut is very fetching.

As a newly appointed paramilitary in the *Sturmabteilung*, Hans is topped off by a little peaked cap reminiscent of his student days. The brown shirt is very well-made with neatly pleated breast pockets, a decorated collar and epaulettes, and it is drawn in at the waist by a buckled leather belt. A matching leather baldric runs from the belt to the right shoulder, should he wish to march up and down and parade with a drum, or a bugle, or a flag, or a flaming torch. The ensemble is set off nicely by a necktie in exactly the same fabric and colour as the shirt. The jodhpur trousers are a slightly darker shade. They bulge at the hips, leaving plenty of wriggle room, even when a practical but optional dagger is worn, and they are gathered in below the knee so that they can slip into beautifully shiny boots that reach above his calves.

All in all, Hans agrees with his wife. He too thinks he looks great.

NSDAP membership card 159,203

Sturmabteilung uniform, 1931

Chapter 21

May 1933
Nuremberg, Germany

Hans is in the papers. The *Fränkischer Kurier* reports that is appointed by the Militant League for German Culture as the main speaker at a mass student rally and book-burning in Nuremburg's main square. He is now working for Alfred Rosenberg, the top Nazi ideologue, who appoints him to Nuremberg City Council with responsibility for making the university toe the party line. With shadows of his own loathing for university life still embedded in his memories, Hans now relishes the task of inciting educated German youth to join in ideological destruction.

Tonight, Hans not only organises the event, but he takes to the podium to lead a sing-song in praise of "flames against the un-German spirit." These flames burn in thirty-four university towns and cities across Germany, and the fires are fuelled by tens of thousands of books. The last time Hans burned a book was on a Hallowe'en, when he turned that Freemason nonsense to ashes in the privacy of his own room. He has come a long way in a short time. Now he enjoys a mass public audience, and most of them are worked up to a vocal and physical frenzy of Nazi slogans and salutes.

Obviously, books by Jewish authors are put to the torch, with the likes of Albert Einstein and Sigmund Freud going up in flames. The bonfire is also fed by Karl Marx, Franz Kafka, Thomas Mann, Victor Hugo, Joseph Conrad, Aldous Huxley, HG Wells, James Joyce, Oscar Wilde, Leo Tolstoy, Vladimir Nabokov, Ernest Hemingway and Heinrich Heine, in which that author writes, "Where they burn books today, they will also burn people in the end." Nobody can yet imagine that the body count will run into millions.

For the past two months Hans works as hard as he can to made sure that target cities are plastered with propaganda posters inciting students to action, so that by now they are mobilised and spoiling for a fight. He would like to take credit for the fact that forty thousand people gather to hear the Minister of Public Enlightenment and Propaganda Joseph Goebbels give a speech declaring, "The era of Jewish intellectualism is now at an end. The future German man will not just be a man of books, but a man of character. It is to this end that we want to educate you. And thus you do well in this midnight hour to commit to the flames the evil spirit of the past." The Nazi war on un-German individual expression has begun. The monster is unleashed.

It is not known if Hans takes personal responsibility for throwing one particular volume on the bonfire. This is a brand new publication by a Belgian named Paul Otlet, and Hans has loathed the Belgians ever since the Walloons waltzed into Germany's industrial heartland the year he quit university. In the publication, Otlet proposes the construction of a gigantic World City, which is to be international, politically neutral and dedicated to peace. It is intended to employ a massive number of workers and help alleviate the unemployment caused by the Great Depression. Hans considers this to be a very dangerous proposal indeed, and it is now added to the flames.

Hans is not only in the German newspapers. The *New York Herald Tribune* columnist Walter Lippmann warns that the book burnings are another step on the road to the Nazis' ultimate destination. He writes for his American readership, "These acts symbolize the moral and intellectual character of the Nazi regime. For these bonfires are not the work of schoolboys or mobs but of the German Government. The ominous symbolism of these bonfires is that there is a government in Germany which means to teach its people that their salvation lies in violence."

student incitement poster 1933

Students preparing for rally, 6 May 1933

bookburners, Germany, 10 May 1933

Chapter 22

June 1933
Oranienburger Straße 79, Berlin, Germany

It is only eight weeks since Adolf Hitler is sworn in as Chancellor of Germany by that old fossil von Hindenburg, and today Hans makes his move. There is plenty of funding to be had in the state coffers, and he aims to get his snout deep into the trough and claim his share. He calls in favours from several Nazi heavyweights including Alfred Baumler, Hans Johst, Hellmuth Langenbucher and Gotthard Urban, and they shift the provincial Book Counselling Centre from where Hans works in Nuremberg to the centre of Berlin. Oranienburger Straße 79 is is a prestigious address, off Unter den Linden near the cathedral and near the synagogue. It is a massive warren of neo-gothic offices, with very small windows and very large egos.

Hans takes over its management, and in a letter to the Nazi Teachers Association he declares his new operational centre as "the unofficial department of the Reich Ministry of Enlightenment and Propaganda." Nobody questions this at the time, so Hans takes it upon himself to order his staff to go and inspect schools and universities and to make sure they follow the party line. He also begins to submit increasing claims for funding.

Before very long, his power-grab comes to the attention of the all-powerful Alfred Rosenberg who fires off a note to say, "If I do not have clarity about your budget by the end of this month, I will apply for the liquidation of your office." Hans now has a blot on his record for empire-building and overstepping the mark, and this will not be for the last time.

But for now, Hans Hagemeyer is doing well. He is in

charge of the Reich Office for the Promotion of German Literature and he is running his own publishing house. His successes include exhibitions called *Eternal Germany*, *Military Germany*, *Political Germany*, *Europe's Fate*, as well as his all-time favourite show called *German Greatness*.

In parallel with Paul Otlet in this same year, his ambition is to create a global resource for "all indirect and direct media of data and literature", albeit of the German persuasion. Hans is committed to this goal, and wants to construct a state library to act as the supreme authority in the organisational structure of the Nazi control of written output.

But unlike Paul Otlet who is struggling to maintain his team at this time, Hans manages to secure four hundred editors at his disposal. He gives daily lectures and his boss Rosenberg publicly boasts that Hagemeyer's department analyses 3,000 manuscripts from the prehistory area alone and that Hans acts as "the Führer's commissioner for the supervision of the entire intellectual and ideological education of the Nazi party".

Hans still simmers with his hatred for schools and universities, and declares that his ambition is to "take over the main principal for all educational literature", but this is a step too far. In particular he steps on the toes of Walter Stang who heads up that particular fiefdom, and the big boss Rosenberg receives a growing number of complaints about Hans. One in particular is from an "unnamed individual" in the Führer's office, with a complaint that lodges an objection to Hagemeyer's status and methods. The complaint is overruled by a direct order from Hitler himself.

It is highly likely that the "unnamed individual" is Philipp Bouhler, former editor of *Der Nationalsozialist* newspaper, and now Commissioner for Cultural Tasks, who happens to be married to Helli Majer, "the most beautiful woman in the Reich Chancellery" and a particular favourite of the Führer.

Bouhler joins the Nazis much earlier than Hans, in fact his membership number is 12. He studies philosophy at university, takes part in the Munich Beer Hall Putsch, is appointed Chief of the Chancellery by Hitler himself, and is responsible for the *Aktion T4* euthanasia monstrosity that murders more than a quarter of a million adults and children who have the audacity to be disabled, deformed or deviant from the Nazi idealised template for humanity. In twelve years time he is arrested by victorious Americans, and commits suicide before he can be brought to trial. The most beautiful Helli also commits suicide, at the age of 33.
    Philipp Bouhler is undoubtedly the main competitor to Hans Hagemeyer when it comes to commandeering the cultural ambitions of the Third Reich, and as chairman of the Official Party Inspection Commission for the Protection of National Socialist Literature, he rivals Hans in believing he knows best what is and what is not suitable for their fellow citizens to read.
    What really irritates Hans is not the fact that Phillip Bouhler is installed as a member of the Reichstag as soon as Hitler takes power, it is the fact that he, Hans Hagemeyer, is not. Hans intends to put this situation right as soon as he can, and he sets about looking for a vacant parliamentary seat knowing that empty seats commonly become vacant in only one of two ways, disgrace or death.

Chancellor Hitler and President Hindenburg, 1933

Nazis take their seats in Parliament

Helli Majer and Philipp Bouhler

Chapter 23

August 1939
Office of Surveillance and Foreign Affairs, Berlin, Germany

Hans receives news of great comfort and joy! He is awarded the illustrious Golden Badge for his services to the Nazi party. Not only that, but he is now promoted to Head of Department just in time for the outbreak of World War Two. His new role seems very straightforward. It is to identify subversive authors and their publications, and then make them disappear. It is not part of his remit to judge whether or not such authors are actually subversive, or even to establish what constitutes subversion in the first place. He is simply obeying orders, which he does with relish and enthusiasm.

To his great satisfaction, he picks up a book with his own name on the cover. The paper, binding and ink all smell fresh from the printer. This is his *Jewish Bibliography*, and it contains an alphabetical list of all Jewish authors and their works. Hans still likes making lists. He carefully places the new book front-face on a shelf behind his desk, so that visitors to his office can view it in pride of place. It stands next to a recent publication which he considers his masterwork, *Europe's Fate in the East – the Battle Against Bolshevism, by Hans Hagemeyer.*

He keeps an album of reviews of the books he authors and edits in his desk drawer and they are universally excellent. This may have something to do with the fact that the reviewers are all appointed by his own department, but a man has to make a living. There are several other books on display with his name on the cover, and he is very proud of them all. Their bindings are expensive and cloth covered, and the cover lettering is nicely embossed with no expense spared. Sales have been good, of course they have, because loyal party members have a duty to buy them even if they don't read them.

On the desk in front of him is a report he is currently working on for the founder of the Gestapo, Hermann Goering. It is still a bit of a mess, but Hans thinks he can knock it into shape without too much trouble. It concerns an investigation into irregularities that appear to exist during the ethnic cleansing of Franconia, and although there is no deadline for submitting it to Goering it will have to be edited by hand before it can be typed up and submitted to the Boss.

"By order of the Reich Chancellor of the Exchequer, issued with the agreement of the Fuehrer's deputy, all party officers, including organisations and attached formations, are forbidden to accept administrative dues, donations, gifts, bequests or material payments of any other kind for the participation of the party in economic tasks, including the transfer of Jewish enterprises to persons of the German race.

From the course of events, one can only assume that the Reich Chancellor of the Exchequer's order was considered not to apply to Franconia, and certain people thought themselves entitled to obtain considerable sums of money in connection with Aryanisation there.

On the night of the 10th November 1938, events took place throughout Germany which I considered to be the signal for a completely different treatment of the Jewish question in Germany. Synagogues and Jewish schools were burnt down and Jewish property was smashed both in shops and in private houses. Towards midday we discussed these events in Gauleiter Streicher's house. We were of the opinion (particularly myself) that we should now act on our own initiative in this respect. I proposed to the Gauleiter that, in view of the great existing lack of houses, the best thing would be to put the Jews into a kind of internment camp. Then the houses would become free in a twinkling and the housing shortage would be relieved, at least in part. Besides that, we would have the Jews under control and supervision.

The Aryanisation was accomplished by the transfer of properties, the surrender of claims, especially mortgage claims, and reductions in buying price. The payment allowed to the Jews was basically 10% of the nominal value. As a justification for these low prices, Holz claimed at the Berlin meeting of the 6th February 1939 that the Jews had mostly bought their property during the inflation period for a tenth of its value.

In the presence of Fink, Koenig informed the Gauleiter of a completed transaction in detail. The Gauleiter gave his complete assent and, in addition, gave the order to transfer the parcel of shares from the account of the banking firm Kohn to the account of Fink at the Dresdner Bank. He further ordered that his name should not be mentioned at all in connection with the transaction. By order of the Gauleiter, Fink withdrew 5,600 Reichsmark from a Stuermer account, and later, also acting for the Gauleiter, he bought the shares of the Mars-Dresdner Bank for the Gauleiter with Stuermer funds.

Gauleiter Streicher likes to beat people with a riding whip, but only if he is in the company of several persons assisting him. Usually the beatings are carried out with sadistic brutality. The best known case is that of Steinruck, whom he beat bloodily in his prison cell. After returning from this scene he said he was relieved and needed to do that again!

Streicher is regarded as extremely brutal. The statements made by Direktor Fink are especially significant. He declared that he was convinced that the Gauleiter would have him bumped off one of these days, as soon as he found out that Fink had told the truth to the investigating commission."

Hans pulls an embossed presentation case towards him and extracts his favourite fountain pen. It is a military edition, even though Hans has never served in the military. A silver Mont Blanc decorated with oak leaves and double Swastika. He twists off the cap, checks the ink and begins to edit the report. A decade later, the report is used as evidence in a trial for war crimes against humanity, and remains as evidence to prove who knew what and when they knew it.

How ironic then, that the books and reports written by Hans Hagemeyer will one day be microfilmed, using the exact camera and projection techniques first proposed by Paul Otlet, and using a similar filing system. This is how the microfilm file begins.

"These seized German records deposited at the World War II Records Division, National Archives, have been microfilmed by the Microfilming Project of the Committee for the Study of War Documents of the American Historical Association. The data sheets are filmed as a target sheet at the beginning of each roll of film, covering 123 rolls of film of records. The terms Serial and Roll refer to the sequence of the film. The Item number is the identification symbol on the original folder. Provenance indicates the archival origin of the documents whose description follows. First Frame gives the frame number of the first page of the folder. Each exposure has been given a frame number consecutively throughout the filming operation. German file numbers, whenever ascertainable, have also been included."

Meanwhile, back in 1939, August ends, September begins, and so does World War II. Hans Hagemeyer has indeed come a very long way from the youth who was working in the fields when the previous war erupted, and this time round he strengthens his intention to exact revenge on the Belgians for the humiliation of its aftermath.

Form and Development of the Reich, by Hans Hagemeyer

Europe's Fate in the East, by Hans Hagemeyer

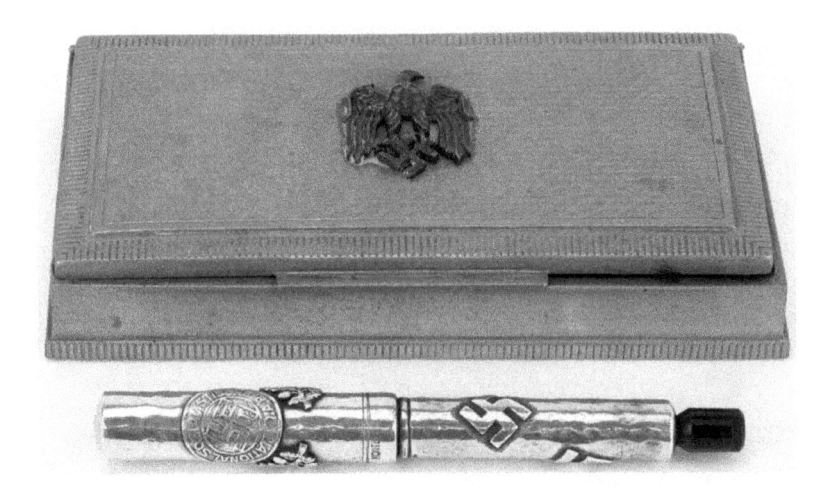

Mont Blanc silver fountain pen with oak leaves and swastikas

10 November 1938, Nuremburg, looting of Jewish books for burning

Chapter 24

January 1940
Office of the Führer's Commissioner, Berlin

Hans is climbing further up the greasy pole. There he is on page 180 of the National Socialist Yearbook for 1940, writ large as *Director for German Literature in the Office of the Führer's Commission for Spiritual and Ideological Instruction of the Nazi Party*. His remit is impressive, and it includes promoting the infamous Strength Through Joy doctrine, along with responsibility for the detailed planning of all the educational work of the Nazi Party.

His Office is set up by Alfred Rosenberg on direct orders from Hitler, but not for the first time things are by no means running smoothly for Hans. There are two other men in the department who pose a threat to him. One is the war hero Gotthard Urban, who occupies the parliamentary seat that Hans covets, and the other is his old enemy and rival Philipp Bouhler who regards German education and literature as his own domain. Hans is well aware of these threats, and he bides his time as he churns out educational and teaching doctrines while he rides the storm.

Hans tries to extend his empire into the area of textbook censorship, but Philipp Bouhler will have none of it, and he rejects the ideas that Hans puts forward as "almost impossible", and "completely useless and senseless." And so it is that Hans is shunted aside for the time being, and fails to get state backing for his ideas of a general cultural policy to take control of all libraries and all the reference books on their shelves.

Suddenly there is talk of him being posted away from Berlin, to be involved in the fate of a dangerously subversive institution currently under threat across the border in Brussels. It is obvious to Hans that Hitler intends to invade Belgium in a matter of weeks, and equally obvious that the Belgians are in no position to put up a fight, so he prepares for the inevitable and gathers what information he can about a so-called world information centre known as the Mundaneum. At the same time, he reminds his boss that he was the first man to instruct Nazi propaganda to be used to infiltrate the reference shelves of their own German libraries. He even slips 39 war books into the top one hundred recommended titles for "Holidays, Travel and Entertainment" for German readers to enjoy.

It is on this day that the German government orders the registration of all Jewish-owned property in Poland. It is also on this day that Philipp Bouhler moves against Hans Hagemeyer, forcing him to retaliate. Hans submits his boldest policy plan to Rosenberg yet, and proposes that all publications, libraries and academic institutions are split into three areas of responsibility. These are Research and Science, Church and Religion, and his own empire of Education.

Hans enlists a bunch of party toadies to back him, by promising them key positions in these proposed new departments. His toadies include the Nordic folklore maniac Matthes Ziegler, the book-burner-in-chief Alfred Baeumler, the closet pan-Europeanist Werner Daitz and the rabid anti-communist Georg Leibbrandt. The plan works, Rosenberg approves it and Hans suddenly finds himself lord of the manor over a sizeable empire. He commands twenty-seven underlings and several hundred "volunteers" as he revels in the title of Rosenberg's Inspector General.

He hones his skills as an orator and takes great pleasure in addressing large audiences of distinguished guests and state hirelings, who dutifully hang on to his poisonous words with rapt attention and then applaud on cue. At the third session of the Reich Office for the Promotion of German Literature he chooses his setting carefully and commandeers the old auditorium of Berlin University with its marble columns, fancy chandeliers and rank upon rank of purple plush seating. His vendetta against the old academic regime does not cool. Prominent on the front row is the University Rector, Professor Doctor Wilhelm Krüger, a Nazi party appointment renowned for sucking up to every high-ranking individual he can find, and Hans is the highest available.

Hans soon quits Berlin and heads West. His first mission is to sort out Rosenberg's new office in Paris, where he is delighted to write a report that details over five hundred libraries successfully handed over to the army High Command. His intention is to harness the power of information available to the French public in exactly the same way that he has achieved in Germany.

And then he moves up to Belgium, where he has plans to make an exhibition of himself. A great exhibition to finally demonstrate the superiority of German culture over the Walloons. And the exhibition site he intends to commandeer is the most prestigious in Belgium's capital city. The *Parc du Cinquanteniare*, home of the great colonial exposition and Human Zoo of 1897, hub of the 1910 World's Fair, site of the *Palais Mondial* World Palace, and more recently home to Paul Otlet's Mundaneum.

Audience listening to Hans Hagemeyer at the third session of the Reich Office for the Promotion of German Literature

Hans Hagemeyer, right, Head of the Reich Office for the promotion of German Literature

Entry to Parc Cinquantenaire before the German invasion

Chapter 25

Krummhübel, South-West Poland
July 1941

The Second World War is going well for Germany this year. Already in 1941 Britain suffers massive destruction from the air, Yugoslavia and Greece are invaded, academics and writers are liquidated all over Poland, and now troops of the Fatherland invade the Soviet Union. Hans believes they all had it coming and that total victory is in sight. Now it really is the time for him to take his game to the highest level.

He is still not yet a member of parliament, which he finds extremely irksome, but today he represents Germany as Chief of Service on Jewish questions in Europe at the anti-Semitic Congress, held in a fancy holiday hotel deep in South-West Poland. It is after midday when the delegates gather for a leisurely late breakfast, and well into the afternoon before Hans delivers his proposals for "the procurement of propaganda material via radio, newspapers, pamphlets, posters, leaflets and rumour."

His fellow delegates represent Spain, Portugal, Italy, Sweden, Denmark, Rumania, Bulgaria, Croatia, Slovakia, Switzerland, and Turkey, several of which are nominally neutral countries.

After Hans outlines his plans for the elimination of Jewry and the obligatory Nazi ideological world domination, he announces that supper will be available at 1930 hours and then "there will be a comradely get-together, and Miss Stein will be available at the hotel to facilitate telephone calls and other communications out of town."

Hans Hagemeyer's plans for the harnessing of global information and knowledge are as ambitious as those of Paul Otlet, but whereas Paul's intentions are always in the causes of peace and international cooperation, those of Hans are always about oppression and control. As such they are two sides of the same coin. A reflection of one another's motivation and achievement, always intertwined but universally opposed.

Hans, once the resentful student, already has his suffocating grip on the education and social thinking of all Germany's schools and universities. He now intends to achieve the same for the rest of Europe. Furthermore, he intends to achieve state control of all public libraries and centres of information, including print and broadcast media. Ultimately, he believes this will lead to the control of knowledge itself, once writers, photographers, editors, publishers and distributors are tamed. He is in the process of proving that when the population is given a single source of approved information then the masses can be influenced to believe anything at all and to act accordingly. There will no longer be any need for conflict, because everyone will strive in unity as a force toward the same goals.

The monitoring of telephone conversations is relatively simple. Initially it requires nothing more than legions of reliable telephone switchboard operators, who by the nature of their jobs already have the ability to listen in to any conversation. Hans thinks he can simplify the eavesdropping process by supplying lists of key words and phrases that automatically trigger an alert if overheard. If that can be done, then even a basically educated individual can be taught what to listen out for when they listen in. It is not known if Miss Stein has been tasked with monitoring the telephone calls made by the delegates to this Congress that Hans is hosting, but it would seem like a golden opportunity not to be missed.

As for newspapers, the war against the independence of the press is already won. Before Hitler comes to power in Germany there are over four thousand dailies and weeklies in circulation, which is higher than any other nation on the planet, but back then the Nazis control less than three per cent of them. So what they do is outlaw their publishers and seize their printing presses, with the excuse that they are preventing an impending communist uprising. It always surprises Hans that people believe what they read in the newspapers, but that is absolutely fine by him.

His boss, Alfred Rosenberg, rises to power as the editor of the People's Observer, which is now run by the party's Eher publishing house, and is the largest mass circulation paper in Germany. The contribution made by Hans and his department is to make sure that copies of the People's Observer and the rabid propaganda weekly *Der Stürmer* are force-fed to the population by making them freely available in every library in the land and on public display on as many street corners as possible. With this as the only source of press reporting and opinion, Hans explains to the other delegates how to achieve the same objective immediately in their own territories.

A far more difficult beast to tame is broadcast media, and Hans is very proud of his country's record when it comes to television and radio. Unlike the free-for-all in other European countries, the German attitude is one of state control from the outset. A regular television service is long established and in place since 1935, ready for the Berlin Olympics when broadcasts are transmitted for eight hours a day. Hardly anyone owns a private television receiver, so most viewings do not take place at home but in public television parlours where communal spirit is encouraged and where it can also be monitored. This is not the case for the mass medium of radio.

While Hans is ensconced in his holiday hotel for the international congress, he communicates with the television pioneer Kurt Wagenführ, who is also a journalist and some-time actor. Wagenführ jokes that Hans has a great face for the movies, and if he ever wants to get into acting then just give him a call. Many years later, when a director named Driefuss is casting a movie, this conversation becomes highly relevant. For now, the news is that Wagenführ has set up the Institute for Broadcasting and Television at Berlin University, and wishes to thank Hans for the support of the Reich Ministry of Public Enlightenment and Propaganda.

The Nazi party has always been aware of the power of radio, and the year that Hitler is sworn in as Chancellor is the year that propaganda minister Joseph Goebbels introduces a crash program to produce the *Volksempfänger*, the People's Radio. It works, it is simple, and above all it is very cheap, because at the subsidised cost of 76 Reichsmarks it undercuts all rival models by a mile. The casing is made of cardboard, cloth and a primitive plastic, adorned with an eagle and a swastika. Everybody wants one. In fact by the time Wagenführ gives Hans the news that their Institute has been set up, 65% of German households are dutifully listening to their *Volksempfänger* people's radios.

It is, of course, a propaganda machine, factory-tuned to receive authorised transmissions approved by the regime. The message on a mass-publicity poster to promote the radio reads, "All Germany hears the Führer on the People's Radio", and the artwork shows an infinite crowd of zombies facing a giant radio monolith. If the listener should ever tire of a mixture of Hitler, bland dance music and cheesy dramas, it is perfectly possible to retune the radio and listen to the BBC. However, doing so is punishable by death.

All Germany does indeed hear the Führer on the people's radio, not only because it is in the home, but it is also piped into factories and offices, and it is wired up to loudspeakers in the streets. Mass media is born, and it is born on a diet of hysteria and fake news.

The prime interest for Hans has always been books, and although his remit is to expand into other media, his personal foible is what is printed between the covers, especially covers with his own name on them. His zeal for book-burning is perverse and powerful, and he is involved in the direct and indirect destruction of millions of volumes. 1,145,500 books are destroyed by the bombing of libraries in Britain. 95% of the contents held in Belarusian libraries are plundered. Belgium loses over a million, Italy two million, Czechoslovakia three million, Poland fifteen million. As for Germany itself, the final tally of loss is uncountable. But Hans Hagemeyer, Chief of Service on Jewish questions in Europe, host of this Krummhübel Congress, does not yet know this.

All Germany hears the Führer on the People's Radio

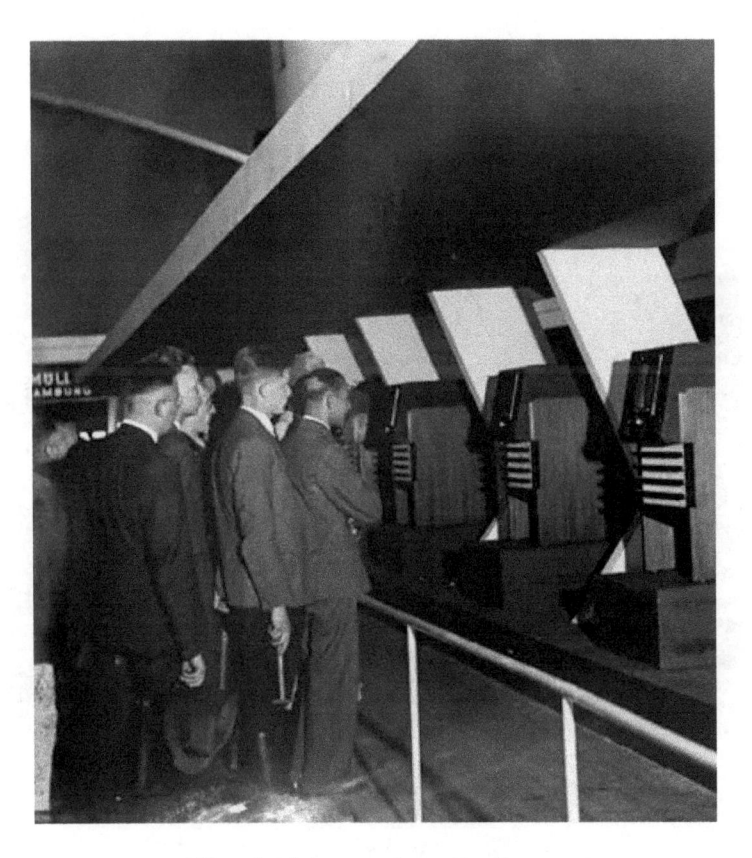

public television parlour, Berlin, 1936

Der Stürmer newspaper street display, 1941

Chapter 26

18 September 1941
The Reichstag, Platz der Republik 1, Berlin

There is something in the air tonight. The Earth is experiencing the most intense magnetic storm that scientists have ever recorded. The demands of war dictate that electrical technology emerges as the central artery for how military communications work. Nor only that, radio is now embedded into the lives of civilians who tune in for a continuous stream of information and for news of victory and defeat.

Multi-coloured auroras dance space ballet across the skies for hours on end. Uncontrolled surges in voltage cables are triggered, causing power cuts and blackouts across the Northern hemisphere. Lightbulbs explode in street lamps, private telephone conversations somehow leak into radio broadcasts, an Allied convoy is exposed to German attack as the night sky turns bright green.

In the World Series, the score between the Brooklyn Dodgers and the Pittsburgh Pirates is still deadlocked at zero-zero in the fourth innings of the game. America is listening to sports commentator Red Barber when the radios go dead. Thousands of baseball fans try to phone and complain, but the phones are dead too. From the State of Maine all the way down to to the State of Florida, people are afraid that the USA is under attack by hostile foreign powers. In fact the USA is indeed under attack, but the attack is from a geomagnetic storm caused by a plasma eruption which is taking place ninety-three million miles away.

Hans Hagemeyer believes the global light-show is very auspicious indeed, because today, after much too long spent waiting in the wings, is the day he finally becomes a member of the German Parliament. The seat he casts his longing eyes on is occupied by none other than Gotthard Urban, his boss at the Margarethen Strasse office of the Führer's Commissioner for all of the spiritual and ideological instruction and education of the Nazi Party, where Hans is in charge of cleaning out libraries and literature of degenerate subversive filth.

Hans first applies for this seat in the Reichstag more than five years before, but always in vain. He is a victim of rivalry, or jealousy, or simple arithmetic, and he has to wait for salvation to arrive in the form of dead man's shoes. Those shoes belong to Urban, the planner of the *Institute for Research into the Jewish Question* with a special remit to confiscate all Jewish libraries. Hans sees this as very much his own fiefdom, but there is nothing he can do about it until Urban finds himself fighting in the German attack ordered by the Führer against Russia, where he is killed in the battle around Lake Ilmen. Now at last the war hero's parliamentary seat is free for Hans to occupy.

Eleven years before, the Nazi Party only holds a paltry 12 seats of the 577 members of parliament. But their voice on the street is far louder than their voice in the Reichstag, and they use it to whip up support through fear and intimidation. The number of seats they win in the 1930 federal elections swells to significant 107 and they use their new-found position as a lever to further power.

All German citizens of twenty-one years and above have the right to vote through a system of proportional representation, and the law states that parliaments are elected every four years. Except they are not, and within months the Nazis make sure they hold the largest number of seats, albeit without any overall majority. So they game the system and table an Enabling Act to ban all opposition parties, with the threat of transport to a concentration camp for anyone voting against them.

Forty-three million votes are cast, three million of these votes are spoiled or left blank, and so it is that forty million votes are recorded as cast for the NSDAP. The result means that the number of seats occupied in the Reichstag are 661 for the Nazis, and absolute zero for anyone else.

Hans intends to exploit this new opportunity to the full in order to expand his own empire, and that expansion of his empire is focussed on his old bête noir, the insignificantly smaller upstart that is Belgium.

1941, Hans Hagemeyer (standing), Member of Parliament

Chapter 27

24 December 1941
Hemelingen, Bremen, Germany

It is Christmas Eve, and the Hagemeyer clan gathers at the old family home to spend the festival of Yule together. Parliament can do without its new member for a few days, and Hans, his wife Erna and their three year-old son Jan travel by rail from Berlin back to Bremen *Hauptbahnhof* where an official car is waiting to take them the short distance to Hemelingen.

Old man Hagemeyer tries to show pleasure when they arrive, but there is pain behind his eyes. Now in his mid-seventies he is not in the best of health. On the other hand, mother is fit as a flea. Sisters Annelise and Margarete are already in situ with four daughters and one son between them, and the house is filled with the noise of children for the first time since the start of the war. In the dining room, the fir tree with its tinsel decorations is topped by a silver swastika which almost touches the ceiling. Red glitter-baubles hang from the branches, each displaying its own swastika logo. Expensively wrapped presents are stacked up beneath the branches, but the wrapping paper is much more traditional and unbranded.

Little Jan, the youngest member of the family, is the apple of his father's eye, and the child's good looks reflect those of both Hans and Erna. One day Jan-Gert Hagemeyer's good looks will earn his fortune, when he becomes the German housewife's heart-throb as television's *Persil Man*. In fact he becomes the family breadwinner for a quarter of a century on the strength of his twinkly eyes, crinkly smile and golden voice. In fifty years time he tires of all the fan-mail, marriage proposals and red-top gossip columns, and becomes a celebrity interviewer. His father Hans is never mentioned, except once, in an interview Jan does with the Ayatollah Khomeini, Supreme Leader of Iran. Meanwhile, here in 1941, it is his father who is the centre of attention. His department is already working on ways to bring Christmas into line with the ideology of Nazism.

Heinrich Himmler hands out *Julleuchter* Yule Lanterns to the SS. These seasonal gifts are hand-decorated pottery candle-holders, pierced with traditional cut-outs so that the flame of the candlelight flickers through, like the pumpkin head lanterns the Americans favour on All Souls Night. These German lanterns each sport the shape of a love-heart, and are mass-produced in the Dachau concentration camp by slave labour. This does not trouble the recipients, but the birth of a Jewish Messiah does trouble many party members, and Hans's boss Alfred Rosenberg is keen to reinstate a new form of paganism to eliminate Jewish and Christian flummery. He even writes a book about it to promote the reputation of a supreme Germanic god, and carefully explains that Santa Claus actually represents Wotan, more commonly known throughout the Aryan nations as the top deity Odin.

Himmler encourages the nation to celebrate the winter solstice as the rebirth of the sun, and his Nazi propaganda department churns out a rebranding campaign for the masses to celebrate in style.

Christmas Eve is to be replaced by Winter Solstice, and Odin is henceforth reincarnated as Solstice Man, who rides a white war-horse, sports a long grey beard and carries a sack full of gifts for all the good children of the Third Reich. The nativity scene is to be updated, with Mary and Jesus depicted as blondes, surrounded by deer and rabbits instead of wise men, shepherds and angels. The press and educational institutions are instructed to replace all references to Christmas trees with pagan Yule trees, and the words of *Silent Night* are changed to exclude all references to the Christian religion.

Hans is still very much involved with educational instruction, and one of his jobs is to promote a new carol called *Great Night of Clear Stars* which is to be sung in schools as a way of eliminating sentimentality and reinforcing national pride at this festive time of year.

And so it is that this evening, with Solstice moved to December the twenty-fourth, Hans gathers the Hagemeyers together around their Yule tree to hold hands, lift their voices and sing the new Party carol together. He hoists little Jan-Gert onto his shoulders, and the boy attempts to join in the song without really understanding what is going on. Three generations of the family look towards the boy with pride and hope for the future as they sing.

Oh great night of clear stars
That reaches down like a bridge
From horizon to horizon
Cradling our hearts.

Great night of great fires
That burn on every mountain
Tonight the earth must renew itself
Like a new-born child!

Mothers, all of you are aflame.
All stars in their rightful place.
Mothers, deep in your own hearts
Beats the heart of the whole wide world.

approved German Christmas card, 1941

Yule tree bauble, 1941

Julleuchter Yule Lantern, 1941

Chapter 28

February 1942
Hoheneichen-Verlag, Wolfratshausen, Munich, Germany.

As the clock ticks away toward the end of the illustrious wartime career of Hans Hagemeyer, Hans does what he does best. He publishes a masterpiece of ambition. It is utterly overblown, and because he is short of time he orders his minions to compile most of the content for him. But it is his name facing the frontispiece and as far as his ego is concerned, that's what counts.

The Hoheneichen publishing house is responsible for producing the first and second editions of this latest Hagemeyer book. It is an institution founded around the time that Paul Otlet's son is killed in the Great War, and it becomes a source of respected text books suitable for education and enlightenment. Within ten years of its foundation it is taken over by the Nazis as a front for publishing their party-line non-fiction. Soon the shackles are removed and the presses are harnessed by Alfred Rosenberg who tasks Hans with turning Hoheneichen into a propaganda factory to indoctrinate schools and universities. Of course the new book is a form of self-publishing for Hans, but it is self-publishing on a grand scale, seeing as Hans runs the entire show and this is the show's biggest ever production.

The title of his magnum opus is *Wife and Mother - the Source of Life of the Nation* and it's a blockbuster. A giant-size, landscape-format, cloth-covered, hernia-inducing doorstopper, with hundreds of illustrations complete with multi-panel fold-outs. The text is meant to arouse pride and to honour German women, but in fact it is a form of gaslighting to keep them unquestioning and subservient, and such text is pulled together by a hack named Herr

Hans-Georg Otto. The photographs are meant to hit the eye and stir the emotion, and again the female form is used as a cypher, curated by Herr Otto Schnieder. But at least Hans finds the time to pen the introduction himself.

He tries to coincide publication of the book with his own birthday, but misses the deadline because the bespoke binding and folding of special concertina pages is far too ambitious. But Hans is nothing if not a smart salesman, and he makes sure his book title is a best-seller by linking it to a major propaganda exhibition of the same name, *Wife and Mother*.

Before the end of the month, Hans intends to head for Belgium, where he is scheduled to launch another propaganda exhibition in the heart of the city of Brussels. He needs to make sure that the existing content occupied by the Mundaneum is stripped out and removed before his arrival, but today the priority is to launch his new book off the back of this *Wife and Mother* exhibition extravaganza.

Celebrity females are ushered in, chaperoned by uniformed officers who makes sure the ladies' delicate sensibilities are shielded from lurid illustrations of German woman corrupted as they cavort and dance with Jews to jazz music performed by negroes. In fact the importance of German women during the Great War merits an expanded chapter in his book of the show, followed by another chapter on the degeneration of those same women under the influence of those decadent French and Belgians who occupy German soil when Hans is in his teenage years. But Hans must omit this section from any escort duties he has today, in order to guard the sensibilities of celebrity females.

Another significant chunk of Hans's book is dedicated to rolls of honour that include printed lists of all 1,800 woman who have the distinction of wearing the Nazi Golden Honour Badge pinned to their proud breasts. This is another smart salesman's ploy to procure a few thousand guaranteed extra sales to the women involved, as well as their friends and extended families. Hans is familiar with the role of women in the Nazi party, but although they are the essence of his exhibition, he has very little direct dealings with them. In fact he regards them as mere appendages to the males. The one exception to this is *Reichsfrauenführerin* Frau Gertrud Scholtz-Klink, and Hans stays very wary of her indeed.

Scholtz-Klink is the boss of the Nazi Women's Bureau, and her slogan is, "German women must work and work. They must work physically and mentally, and they must renounce all luxury and pleasure." This is total hypocrisy on her part, because she lives in the lap of luxury. But she is the biggest influencer in the land, and female party members do her bidding *en masse*. One of her hobbies is gawping at women who fall foul of the regime and find themselves rotting in concentration camps. One of her other hobbies is getting rid of husbands, and when she meets Hans at the exhibition he is well aware that she is getting shot of Husband Number Three and on the lookout for a replacement.

Hitler is close to her in several ways, so Hans is not only wary, he is also on his best behaviour. According to *Time* magazine, "Fifty thousand women and girls, marshalled by hard-bosomed Gertrude Scholtzklink the Number One Female Nazi, hailed Herr Hitler with bursts of wild, ecstatic cheering which was kept up for the whole forty-five minutes that he addressed them. 'There are some things only a man can do!' cried this Apotheosis of the Little Man. 'I exalt women as the most stable element in our Reich because a woman judges with her heart, not with her head! I would not be here now had not women supported me from the very beginning. We deny the Liberal-Jew-Bolshevik theory of women's equality because it dishonours them! A woman, if she understands her mission rightly, will say to a man, 'You preserve our people from danger and I shall give you children.'"

Hans only reads *Time* magazine for research purposes,

of course, and he does not mention her global fame as he shows her around his exhibition.

"Reichfrauenführerin."

"Come now Hans, why so formal? This is not a state occasion, you may call me Gertrud."

"It is a pleasure to welcome you to this celebration of women representing every province of the Reich, and especially the Party *Frauenschaft* and *Deutsches Fruaenwerk* which you lead so ably. I am organising another exhibition in Brussels, to demonstrate our German women's achievements as an example to other ..."

"Thank you Hans. But what special features do you have for me here and now in this exhibition? I have such a busy, busy schedule today."

"Yes, well, in the next room there are women's achievements in sculpture and art."

"What sort of achievements are those?"

"Achievements as models. I mean, as muses, achievements as muses. And of course a woman's duties in raising children ..."

"In accordance with the racial laws."

"Yes, all in accordance with what you have been, um, what you have declared ..."

"Faith and Beauty."

"Precisely. Faith and Beauty. And women working in factories, and the Air Raid Protection Service. But the main emphasis we demonstrate is women as the source of the life of our German Nation. So you see ..."

"Who is depicted in that photograph over there?"

"My apologies. Perhaps the light is a somewhat harsh on the picture frame, making it a little difficult to distinguish. That is Frau Klara Pötzl ..."

"Ah, of course it is. The Führer's mother. How very appropriate"

The Mother's Cross Award

Wife and Mother exhibition 1942, Hans Hagemeyer left, Reichsfrauenführerin Gertrud Scholtz-Klink second-right

Frau und Mutter, published by by Hans Hagemeyer 1942

Chapter 29

March 1942
32 Rue du Châtelain, Brussels, Belgium

The ghost of the Mundaneum remains shuttered and locked inside the *Palais du Cinquantenaire*, once the heartbeat of Brussels but now stifled. Day after day, Paul Otlet hopes for a miracle, but the miracle does not come. The government promises Paul new locations for his Mundaneum, but the promises are broken almost as soon as they are made because every suitable site is requisitioned in preparation for a war.

When Germany does invade Belgium the fears become a reality. Enemy troops occupy Brussels and requisition the *Palais du Cinquantenaire*. They intend to strip it of all vestiges of the Mundaneum. In desperation, and with a final approval from Cato, Paul seeks permission to take over an abandoned university building near the Parc Leopold, but he is barely able to move a fraction of his life's work into a space with no heat and no prospect of funds. Now he faces total defeat, spiritually and financially. The wreckage of the Mundaneum is left to rot in a building formerly used by the Raoul Warocqué Institute of Anatomy. A caretaker leaves food for the cats that feed on the mice that infest the place.

Eggert Reeder is appointed Head of the Administrative Staff of the Military Governor of Belgium, and becomes directly responsible for the elimination of "Jewish, Bolshevik and Freemason influence" from the Belgian economy. Reeder is determined to demonstrate the superior civilisation of the Reich to the Belgians and he turns to Hitler's ideologue Alfred Rosenberg for inspiration.

Rosenberg tasks his all-powerful department to come up with ideas, and on 9th September 1940 a member of his staff draws up a plan for a grand propaganda exhibition of

German achievements. He calls it "a living source of our culture and civilisation", and he proposes that it should be staged in the *Palais du Cinquantenaire*. The name of this staff member is Hans Hagemeyer, and the site is where the bulk of Paul Otlet's Mundaneum is still locked away.

Eventually, Hagemeyer gets the go-ahead direct from Rosenberg, who personally visits Brussels during a tour of the largest abandoned Masonic organization in Belgium, and he notes triumphantly that Hitler wants all pre-1933 archives to be seized. He then sets up headquarters at 32 rue du Châtelain, to administer the seizure of any and all archives that he fancies. His office is not far from the run-down mansion which is still home to Paul Otlet, now faded and frail.

The Nazi regime keeps meticulous records, and the Rosenberg taskforce lists 1,232 crates of Mundaneum archives, books, indexes and data, all appropriated, looted or dumped, along with over 250,000 books shipped off the site. In total, sixty-three tons of material is trashed and removed from the Mundaneum. The remaining dusty rooms, filled with index cards, files and records, are boarded up because they are not considered to be worth refurbishing. Millions of items of microfilmed data are simply left to rot. The site is prepared and made ready for the Hagemeyer propaganda show.

But at the inauguration of the *Great German Exhibition* on 16 March 1942, Hans Hagemeyer makes a mistake. In his welcome speech, he refers to the geographical framework of Belgium, and the "Belgian aspects of our work." And he specifically uses the word *Vorland*, meaning frontier, or foreshore, whereas the official party line is that the territory known as Belgium is to be referred to as part of the Reich. This black mark is made against Hans Hagemeyer by Hitler's propaganda supremo Joseph Goebbels, and it is a black mark that soon comes back to haunt Hans, but not quite yet.

It is a windy morning, but otherwise peaceful in the invaded capital city of Brussels. Paul does not ride the tram for the one stop between his old front door and Hagemeyer's new office. He walks the 550 metres to Rue du Châtelain, painfully and with the aid of a stick. He anticipates that the German will keep him waiting, but this is not the case. In fact Paul is promptly ushered in to the Nazi's office. The two men face one another for the first and last time.

"Ah, Monsieur Otlet, I have been expecting you. I understand that you speak German"

"Good morning, Mein Herr. Yes, I speak German. My first wife was from Berlin and I have travelled throughout your country. I trust you find my country to your liking."

The joke is not lost on Hans, who flutters his hand in a gesture of amusement. "Very good. It seems you wish to make a request regarding the content of the so-called Mundaneum collection, formerly housed in the *Palais du Cinquantenaire*."

Hans opens a folder on the desk in front of him and extracts a single sheet of typescript. Paul already knows the situation is hopeless, but he has promised La Fontaine that he will face their enemy and appeal to a better nature that they both know does not exist. But a promise is a promise and he will go through the motions anyway. His old friend is dying, but his will is indomitable, and Paul will not go against it. The Nazi looks at the old man and then sets out his stall.

"Regarding the content and documentation system of the so-called Mundaneum collection, there is irrefutable evidence that your collaborator in amassing this material is the former member of the Belgian Parliament, namely Senator Henri La Fontaine, and that you come here on his instructions. Is that correct Monsieur Otlet?"

"That is correct, Herr Hagemeyer."

"Was Senator La Fontaine, the former member of the Belgian Parliament, a member of the Socialist Party, and was he also President of the so-called Internationale Union?"

"Yes. That is also correct, Herr Hagemeyer."

"Thank you, Monsieur Otlet. I now ask you, did you collaborate with Senator La Fontaine to found the so-called Internationale Union. Is it correct that you did that, Monsieur Otlet?"

"Yes, this information is in the public record, but it has nothing to do with your removal of material from the *Palais du Cinquantenaire*, and subsequent ..."

"Your collaborator Henri La Fontaine, is he a high-ranking Freemason?"

"What? Yes, I believe he is, but I fail to see... "

Paul pauses mid-sentence. He stares at Hans, then he says, "Herr Hagemeyer, may I ask you a question?"

"Of course."

"Yes? Thank you. You used the expression *documentation system* just now. Am I correct in thinking that you are aware this entire concept and terminology was invented by me? Do you know of my work?"

Hans rises. "Yes, Monsieur Otlet, I am somewhat familiar with your achievements and your declared motivations. Your information system has implications of which I am aware and you must know that it has no place in the New Order. That is an end to the matter, however before you leave, may I ask you another question in turn?"

Paul responds with a sigh, but does not speak, waiting for Hans to do so.

"Are you aware of my own pioneering work in the sphere of libraries and indexing, Monsieur Otlet?"

"I cannot say that I am, Mein Herr. The reason I am here is because I am denied access to the bulk of my life's work in the sphere of libraries and indexing, which has been boarded up by your occupation forces and which is degrading day by day."

"You are referring to the enterprise formerly housed in the *Palais du Cinquantenaire*?"

"No, Mein Herr, I am referring to all the materials that still remain there, and I am asking you for permission to access these materials so that they can be taken to a place of safety."

"I am afraid that is impossible, Monsieur, for the sake of security of my own vitally important exhibition. The content of your Mundaneum has been carefully packed in crates and stored under my personal supervision, and I can assure you that in due course everything will be examined and processed in accordance with our guidelines regarding the best interests of all citizens of the Reich, including our Belgian territories."

Hans jerks his torso towards Paul in what he intends to be a gesture of intimidation, but Paul does not react at all. There is a long silence between the two men, until Hans breaks it.

"I understand that there was a time when you attempted to construct machines for the encoding and decoding of human speech. Is this true, Monsieur Otlet?"

Paul realises that this Nazi is well informed and by no means stupid, and that he needs to choose his words very carefully. Eventually he responds.

"Yes, it is true. There was a time when I proposed such things, but they came to nothing. They were simply ideas. They were plans, or rather hopes of plans for a way of creating ..."

"Of creating what?"

"Perhaps, perhaps some form of automated ..."

"Automated monitoring?"

"No, Herr Hagemeyer, not monitoring. Not monitoring, but an automated system for the exchange of knowledge and information. Remotely. Freely."

"And it truly came to nothing?"

"That is so. I am sorry to say that it came to nothing."

"Do you believe it can be possible, that scientists are able to achieve such things? Ever?"

"I am not sure I understand what you are asking, Herr Hagemeyer."

"I am asking if you think we can ever develop an automated form of communication, Monsieur Otlet, where knowledge can be remotely transmitted and exchanged and monitored by machines? Do you think that given enough resources and with your knowledge you could ever achieve this?"

"No, Herr Hagemeyer, I do not believe this will ever be possible. The human mind, our human communication, can never be replicated artificially. Such devices are impossible."

Hans has always believed this to be true, but he can only imagine the power such devices would give their controllers. The two men stare at one another for what seems like an overlong time, and then Hans says, "I have noted your request and it will be dealt with in due course. Thank you for your time."

Of course, Hans does not note any requests because he does not give Paul the courtesy of explaining them further. The interview is over and Hans gestures for Paul to leave, but his tone has become softer and he almost feels a bizarre sort of sympathy for this sad old man. He observes that during their short meeting, behind the wire-framed spectacles, Paul Otlet does not blink once. He is sad, and he is old, but he is also an unusual man. Hans Hagemeyer does not raise his arm in the habitual Nazi salute, but neither does Paul Otlet extend his own hand in ritual courtesy. They exchange a brief nod of the head.

Paul mutters, "I will convey our conversation to Senator La Fontaine, and he will no doubt be in contact with your superiors."

In response Hans does not twist the knife, but he simply confirms what Paul already knows, and says, "In the context of the Mundaneum apparatus and its content, Monsieur Otlet, I have no superiors."

And in response to this statement of finality from

Hans, Paul turns around, leaves the building and simply walks away. Hans waits a while before reopening the folder on his desk and uncovering the list of questions prepared by him to ask the great man. Questions which he will now never ask. Hans likes lists, and this one contains something very special, copied from a text published by Paul Otlet some years ago.

"Operation number One – the transformation of sound into writing.

Operation number Two – the reproduction of this writing into as many copies as are needed.

Operation number Three – the creation of data in such a way that each item of information has its own identity, and can be retrieved as necessary.

Operation number Four – a classification number assigned to each specific item of information.

Operation number Five – the automatic classification and filing of this data by machine.

Operation number Six – the automatic retrieval of data for consultation, presented either direct to the enquirer or via machine, enabling written additions to be made.

Operation number Seven – the mechanical manipulation at will of all the listed items of information, in order to obtain new combinations of facts, new relationships of ideas, and new operations carried out with the help of numeric code.

The technology fulfilling these seven requirements will create a mechanical collective brain.

Anyone will be able to consult information remotely from afar, expanded or limited to the desired subject, projected on their individual screen.

Thus, in their armchair at home or in their place of work, anyone will be able to contemplate the whole of creation, or any part of it."

Hans stares at the sheet of paper before relaxing the tension in his neck and shoulders. He moves to the window, and watches an old man moving painfully with the aid of a stick along Rue du Châtelain. And then, silently, he uses the back of his hand to wipe something from his eye.

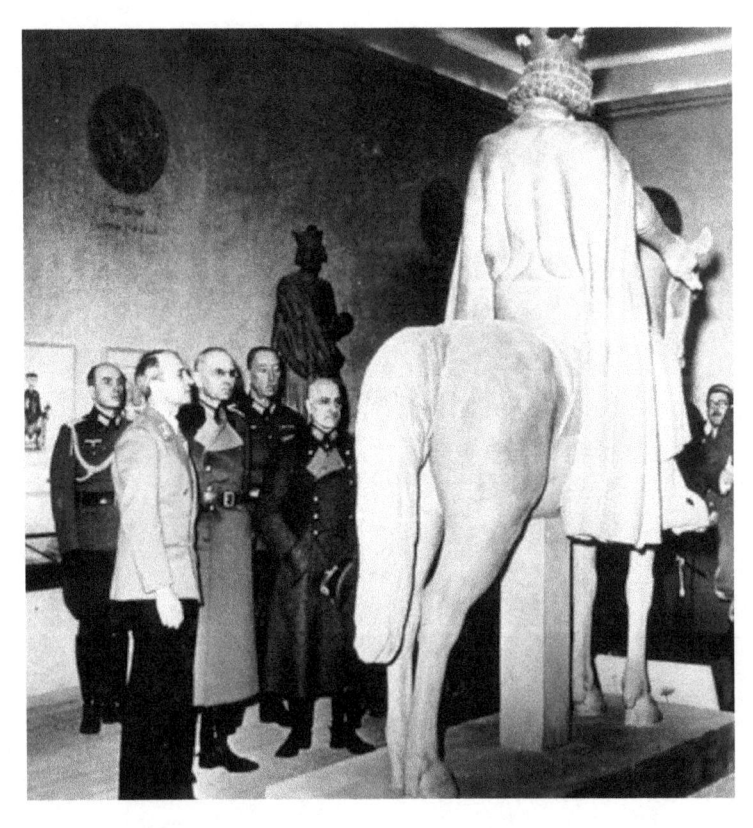

Hans Hagemeyer, 2nd left, opening of Great German Exhibition, former site of the Mundaneum, Brussels, 1942

Chapter 30

19 November 1944
Einsatztab Reichsleiter Rosenberg, Berlin

The grand plans for the city of *Germania* are never to be realised. It is one year to the day since four hundred Lancaster bombers attack Berlin. Firestorms break out across the German capital, shattering windows, scorching furniture, blistering plaster, destroying whole residential quarters of the city. The iconic Kaiser Wilhelm Memorial Church is reduced to smouldering stumps, the magnificent Charlottenberg Palace is in ruins, the beloved Berlin Zoo is a bedlam of chaos and panic. The destruction of homes and landmarks is collateral damage unleashed by His Majesty's Royal Air Force. The embassy quarter is destroyed, the Ministry of Munitions and the Waffen SS College, the old Imperial Guard Barracks, all gone. And the transport system is crippled. So Hans walks to work.

Hans is not a happy man. Ever since he takes over from Matthes Ziegler, he spends two years building a meticulous database of international loot for his boss Alfred Rosenberg. He organises files, lists, photographs, places and dates, in fact he compiles a complete record of everything taken from Freemasons, Jews, Communists, and other enemies, plundered from Ukraine to Belgium and everywhere in between. There are hundreds of thousands of such items, and Hans makes sure they all get sorted, catalogued, valued and accounted for. It is the greatest list of his career. The only comparable archive he knows of is the delusion that was once called the Mundaneum, and that is long gone.

So it comes as a complete shock to Hans when Rosenberg orders him to be relieved of this magnificent database duty and replaced as head of "literature cultivation" by the militarist Bernhard Payr, and Hans responds with a knee-jerk reaction. He sends a letter of complaint to Heinrich Himmler in order to set out his record of achievements and evidence of success. Hans offers to do whatever is necessary to get himself reinstated.

This is a mistake. The war is not just going badly, the war is a disaster. Everybody except the Führer seems to accept that the reckoning is coming, and as the main architect of the holocaust against the Jews, Himmler has other things to occupy his mind about what the future holds. The letter Himmler receives from Hans is an irritation he can do without.

Himmler refers to a note in the records of the Nazi Party law firm saying that none other than Joseph Goebbels thinks Hans Hagemeyer is unsuitable for being in charge of any so-called "state powers", but of course Hans is unaware of this and today things take a direction from which there is no going back. Goebbels is still in charge of German propaganda and has taken direct powers to run the mess that is Berlin, but in his heart of hearts even Goebbels knows the war is lost, and he lashes out. The data that Hans has compiled is not just a complete record of Nazi looting, it is sufficient proof to condemn them all for international crimes against humanity, and Hans is in effect barred from access to his own archive. In a bizarre parallel to the fate of the Mundaneum, all the immaculately compiled records are unceremoniously crated, loaded up and removed from the site. One day certain of these files reappear as evidence at the Nuremberg trials for war crimes.

And now, to put the final nail in the career coffin, Hitler's personal secretary Martin Bormann gets in on the act. Bormann not only questions the capabilities of Hans Hagemeyer, but he puts it on record that Hans is an underperformer, recommending he should be "put to another use."

Soon insults begin to fly and reach the level of kindergarten name-calling, until Rosenberg loses his patience and issues his own order to scupper Hans's work. As often happens in these situations, it is not the great crime that brings down a monster, it is the trivia. There is gossip that a university appointment has been handed out to one of Hagemeyer's circle in an act of cronyism instead of one of suitability. Careful not to suffer another knee-jerk reaction, Hans makes a bad situation worse, this time by not responding to the criticism immediately, and he is summoned into Rosenberg's presence.

"Hagemeyer, I wish to remind you that in the past one and a half years I have tasked you with only two things. The implementation of the anti-Jewish congress in that Polish holiday hotel and the compilation of records pertaining to the confiscation of properties belonging to enemies of the state."

"Yes, and it ..."

"So why are you involved with trivia like who occupies a university Physics Chair?"

Hans is completely wrongfooted by this.

"But these university matters, they have always been part of my ..."

"Especially when such positions are to be awarded only to opponents of theories posited by the Jew Albert Einstein."

"Yes, but I have established a centre of anti-Jewish physicists in a recently acquired property in Eppenhain, and soon this ..."

"I am cancelling that project here and now. Do you understand Dienstleiter Hagemeyer. Do you understand?"

"Yes, of course, Reichsleiter. Yes, of course, I completely understand."

Hans does not even hear the axe rise or fall before the blow is struck.

"Under the instruction of Secretary Bormann, your department is to be dissolved. You will hand over your offices and files to Dienstleiter Heinrich Härtle. Thank you for your efforts, you are dismissed of all duties and you are free to leave. Heil Hitler!"

    Hans does not protest. In fact he does not respond at all. It is always going to end like this. And now, as the inevitable finally happens, Hans Hagemeyer simply leaves the room, wanders out onto the street and he too walks away.

central Berlin after RAF air raids of December 1944

Destruction of the Hagemeyer archives 1944

Alfred Rosenberg 1944

Hans Hagemeyer 1944

Chapter 31

22 December 1944
Etterbeek Cemetery, near Brussels, Belgium

There is an orderly cemetery in Etterbeek. It is near the site where Napoleon suffers defeat in the Battle of Waterloo, and it is inland from the battlefield where Paul Otlet's younger son Jean loses his life a century after Waterloo in the First World War. And now, on this day, another battle rages. It is one of the most deadly campaigns in American history and the bloodiest single battle fought by the US army in this Second World War. In years to come it is called the Battle of the Bulge.

The Germans are on the offensive, with orders to use their mechanised forces to move North and take Antwerp harbour before the Allies can bring their superior air power into play. This Christmas the weather is bad, and the 101st Airborne Division is grounded. General George Patton is bogged down near Bastogne. General Heinrich von Lüttwitz leads the force that traps the Americans, and he sends an ultimatum to the American commander Anthony McAuliffe, which reads as follows.

"To the U.S. Commander of the encircled town of Bastogne. The fortune of war is changing. The American forces have been encircled by strong German armoured units. More German armoured units have crossed the river. Our forces near Ortheuville have taken Marche and reached St. Hubert. Libramont is in German hands. There is only one possibility to save your encircled American troops from total annihilation, and that is honourable surrender. In order to think it over, a term of two hours will be granted beginning with the presentation of this note. If this proposal should be rejected, German Artillery Corps and six heavy AA Battalions are ready to obliterate your troops. The order for your destruction will be given immediately after two hours. The most serious civilian losses caused by this artillery fire will not correspond with your well-known American humanity. The German Commander."

McAuliffe replies to von Lüttwitz immediately with the following communication.

"To the German Commander from the American Commander: nuts!"

In the US Army parlance of the day, the colloquial meaning of the word nuts can refer to the testicular sack.

On the outskirts of Brussels, in Etterbeek cemetery, with the distant sound of heavy gunfire rolling in from the South, a man is laid to rest beneath the dirt. His mortal remains are seventy-six years old. There is no death certificate because the office of the registrar is a casualty of the artillery. A terracotta pot is placed close to the grave, containing some droopy chrysanthemums culled from a local doner's damaged greenhouse. By contrast, a freshly-dug adjacent grave is covered in white flowers, left there by mourners attending a previous burial. Today, two women stand there in the cold. They are Cato Van Nederhasselt and Léonie La Fontaine, both now widows. Only a handful of other mourners are present at this internment, partly because the deceased is a forgotten man and partly because news of his death is stifled by war.

The previous week, he completes the twelfth session of a six day course on documentation which he has devised for the students at the university where the wreckage of the Mundaneum is housed. Then he returns home, works until seven in the evening and dies.

The grave's reference coordinate is noted as 21-8090-486. The memorial features five square grey stone slabs rising above a plinth. There is a stylised globe on the top, half-covered by a chiselled shroud. Carved into the base are the words *Il ne fut rien sinon mundanéen*, which may be translated by a casual observer as, "he was nothing but mundane." A more careful translation could read, "He was nothing but Mundanian". But the intended meaning is surely more like, "He embraced the whole world." In any case, the words are ambiguous.

There is a dominant inscription above these ill-chosen words in capital letters, and it is the name of the man who lies beneath. Today, in the age of mobile communications and the Internet, the first name is half worn away by time and neglect. The second name is still legible. It reads OTLET.

Paul Otlet 1868-1944, untended grave

Chapter 32

November 1958
Veluwe Forest, Gelderland, Belgian-Dutch border

Three men relax under the winter trees, smoking cigarettes and talking. They are actors in a movie, and they are playing the parts of a bunch of German commandos who are led by the fanatical son of an evil Nazi General. They are kitted out in American army uniforms, and the reason for this is because they are supposed to be in disguise. The title of the movie is *The Last Blitzkrieg* and it is soon hailed by critics and cinemagoers alike as a stinker. It is being directed by Arthur Driefuss for a Dutch studio called Cinetone. Driefuss is Jewish as are many of the crew. The action is set in 1944 Belgium, which is not so long ago and not so far away. The movie is to be released by Columbia Pictures on the box-office reputation of the lead actor Van Johnson, who is sharing cigarettes and conversation with the other two actors. One of them is a gangly thirty-year old from Fort Wayne called Dick York, the other is a middle-aged German from Saxony called Hans. They are talking about the future of television.

The first actor, Van Johnson, doesn't serve in World War Two because doctors have put a large metal plate in his head after he smashes his skull in a car accident. Instead of fighting in the war, he becomes a matinee idol for Metro-Goldwyn-Meyer, playing all-American boy-next-door heroes. In six months time he will be offered the starring role of Eliot Ness in a TV series called *The Untouchables*, which he will turn down because he fails to see the future of popular television. The role is given to his friend Robert Stack instead. Today Johnson is playing the part of Hans

Von Kroner, a would-be good guy mixed up in the last German offensive of the war in Belgium. His mission is to command a group of English-speaking Germans and infiltrate American units fighting in the Ardennes region. His men are to create panic and confusion among the retreating Yanks. They are also ordered to deliver fake HQ orders and commit acts of sabotage. Kapow!

The second actor, Dick York, is too young to fight in World War Two. He begins his career at the age of fifteen and appears in hundreds of radio shows before hitting the Broadway stage. In six months time he makes another war movie with the lofty Gary Cooper and the equally lofty Rita Hayworth, and during a film stunt he suffers a catastrophic back injury. Unlike Van Johnson, Dick York clearly sees the future of popular television, and in a couple of years time when he is offered a supporting role in *The Untouchables*, he grabs it. Despite an addiction to painkillers, he goes on to become a global TV favourite playing the bewildered husband in the long-running sitcom *Bewitched*, for which he gets an Emmy nomination.

The third actor, Hans, is exactly the right age to serve in World War Two, so he is well-suited to play a German Nazi Lieutenant in *The Last Blitzkrieg*. He gets on well with the crew, and he knows the area well, all the way from here in the forest up to the target city of Brussels. In fact he was stationed in Brussels only a few years earlier.

Hans Hagemeyer is the former head of the Reich Office for the promotion of German values and the former representative of the Führer for ideological training, with instructions to activate the fight against the Jews and corrupt the souls of German youth. He too sees the future of popular television and has already set his twenty-year-old son on the pathway to a TV career. In fifteen years time his son Jan-Gert Hagemeyer achieves fame as the creator and anchor-man of the *Persil Washes Whiter* television advertising campaign, and becomes the heart-throb of several million post-war German housewives.

Hans is very interested in the future of mass media and asks the two Americans about a project called ARPA which is just launched by the US Department of Defense, but they have never heard of it. ARPA employs over two hundred scientists and their mission is to create a communications network between several computers in different locations. There comes a time when this is claimed as the origin of the internet, but that claim is false. The project has echoes of one that Hans remembers being invented back in the 1890s by that sad old man he kicked out his office while he was stationed in Brussels. He recalls the geriatric face with a downy white beard and unblinking eyes. But for the life of him, he cannot fully remember the old man's name.

*****

On 10 October 1993, Hans Hagemeyer dies peacefully at home in his own bed, a respected pensioner in the community, aged 94.

Hans Hagemeyer, acting in 'The Last Blitzkrieg' 1958

*Paul Otlet, a forgotten man, in his final year
with a model of the Cité Mondiale*

AUTHOR'S AFTERWORD

In the summer of 1969, I went with a small group of architectural students to visit a manicured estate in the Hampshire countryside called Brockwood Park. There we met Jiddu Krishnamurti, an old man who in his youth had been acclaimed by legions of followers as a Messianic figure known as The World Teacher. What the Messiah was doing holed up in a swanky private school just off the A272 trunk road is as much a mystery to me now as it was then. After a lecture on peace and love, Krishnamurti invited questions from the awkwardly cross-legged youths gathered at his feet, and one of my chums asked him to name the person he admired the most. I remember there was a long pause before the guru closed his eyes and named someone called Paul Otlet. I had never heard of Paul Otlet, but I dutifully wrote down the name and then forgot all about it.

In the summer of 1985, I spent time with the General Secretary of the Campaign for Nuclear Disarmament and President of the International Peace Bureau, Monsignor Bruce Kent. Most of our time was taken up playing video games, but that's another story. Anyway, I asked him to name his heroes and among the usual suspects he cited someone called Paul Otlet. The name meant nothing to me, and once again I wrote it down but forgot all about it.

In the summer of 1993, I was commissioned by a Belgian software company to create an artificial intelligence that lived inside a pocket computer. The company was run by my friend Jacques Chapon, who insisted that the increasingly popular phenomenon known as the World Wide Web had been invented by a local Belgian lad. I laughed at the idea, but then Jacques introduced me to a story about a man named Paul Otlet saying, "Mel, he was like you: a great one for ideas, but rubbish at business." This time round, I started to gather what information I could to piece together a truly remarkable story, and it was during this process that I came across the name Hans Hagemeyer, who was still alive but only just. Then I forgot all about both of them for another thirty years.

And now, I find myself the same age that poor old Paul Otlet was when he died a forgotten man, and I find the time to write this book in order to try and set the record straight. Here's hoping it does.

Thank you Jiddu Krishnamurti, thank you Bruce Kent, thank you Jacques Chapon, and thank you for reading this.

Mel Croucher

Paul Otlet (left) and Jiddu Krishnamurti, 1926

PHOTOGRAPHIC AND PICTORIAL IMAGES

• Cover images and frontispiece. © Mel Croucher 2024.
• Otlet/ Hagemeyer combined key image. © Mel Croucher. 2024.
• Author's image. © Mel Croucher. 2024.

Chapter 1
• Inauguration day Brussels tramway. Photographer unknown, Musée du transport urbain Bruxellois. 1874. Public Domain.
• Paul Otlet, bébé dans les bras de sa mère Marie Van Mons, 1868. Public Domain.
• Paul Otlet à l'âge de 8 ans. Photographe Dupont, Bruxelles, 1876. Public Domain.

Chapter 2
• Leibniz card index, Vincent Placcius, De arte excerpendi, 1689. Houghton Library, Harvard University. Public Domain.
• Lycée Louis-le-grand, 1891 postcard, photographer unknown. Public Domain.
• Anatole Baily, librarian, 1881, photographer unknown. Public Domain.
• Melvil Dewey *A Classification and Subject Index, for Cataloguing and Arranging the Books and Pamphlets of a Library*, 1876. Lockwood & Brainard Company. Open Library. Public Domain.

Chapter 3
• Rotary dial telephone, 1891, Siemens und Halske AG, Berlin. Public Domain.
• Henri La Fontaine, 1891, Géruzet Frères, Bruxelles. Public Domain.

• Paul Otlet, Photographe Dupont, Bruxelles, 1891. Public Domain.
• the Otlet family and friends dine out, 1890, photographer unknown. Public Domain.

Chapter 4
• Paul Otlet's season ticket, 1897, Tervueren template. Public Domain.
• Vue du Palais du Cinquantenaire lors de l'Exposition universelle, 1897, photographer unknown. Public Domain.
• Souvenir postcard of the Colonial Palace human zoo, 1897, publisher unknown. Public Domain.
• the Otlet mansion, 1897, photographer unknown. Public Domain.

Chapter 5
• Staircase of the Jews, Hotel Ravenstein, 1895, photographer unknown. Public Domain.
• Melvil Dewey, 1895, University of Winsconsin-Madison Information Collection. Public Domain.
• Opening of the International Federation for Information and Documentation, 1895, photographer unknown. Public Domain.
• Otlet development site at Westende, 1895, Archive Centre of the French Community of Wallonia, Brussels. Photographer unknown. Public Domain.

Chapter 6
• Eduard Otlet memorial photograph, 1907. Féderation Wallonie Bruxells de Belgique, centre d'archives, Mons. Public Domain.
• Otlet father and sons visiting their mines, 1900, photographer unknown. Public Domain.
• Paul Otlet the unwilling businessman 1906, photographer unknown. Public Domain.

• Microphotography, by Paul Otlet and Robert Goldschmidt, 1906, Institut International de Bibliographie, publication No.81, Harvard University Library, Public Domain.

Chapter 7
• Logo and organisational diagram of the Central Office of International Associations, 1907, Union of International Associations collection, Rue Washington, Brussels. Public Domain.
• International Peace Conference, The Hague 1907, photographer unknown. Public Domain.

Chapter 8
• Mundaneum Team, Mundaneum data-processing, Mundaneum telegraph room, Mundaneum floor plan, Mundaneum micro-photography exhibition room. 1905 to 1913, all images from Mundaneum Wallonia-Brussels Federation collection research archives and European Commission for Culture and Creativity. Public Domain.

Chapter 9
• Cato van Nederhesselt Otlet, 1919, photographer unknown. Public Domain.
• Mathilde La Fontaine, 1932, Mundaneum Wallonia-Brussels Federation collection research archives and European Commission for Culture and Creativity. Public Domain.
• Léonie La Fontaine, Happy Hour, 1902, Mundaneum Wallonia-Brussels Federation collection research archives and European Commission for Culture and Creativity. Public Domain.
• Léonie La Fontaine and her political allies, 1900, Mundaneum Wallonia-Brussels Federation collection research archives and European Commission for Culture and Creativity. Public Domain.
• Mademoiselle Poels at work in the Mundaneum, Mundaneum Wallonia-Brussels Federation collection

research archives and European Commission for Culture and Creativity. Public Domain.
• Marie-Louise de Bauche at work in the Mundaneum, Mundaneum Wallonia-Brussels Federation collection research archives and European Commission for Culture and Creativity. Public Domain.
• Poels, de Bauche and Mundaneum assistants, Mundaneum Wallonia-Brussels Federation collection research archives and European Commission for Culture and Creativity. Public Domain.
• King Albert of Belgium and Queen Elizabeth of Bavaria visit the Yser Front, 1914, Jean-Pol Grandmont, commons.wikimedia.org. Public Domain.

Chapter 10
• Marcus Garvey, 1924, US Library of Congress. Public Domain.
• William Du Bois, 1921, photographer unknown. Public Domain.
• Second Pan-African Congress, Palais Mondial, 1921. Mundaneum Wallonia-Brussels Federation collection research archives and European Commission for Culture and Creativity. Public Domain.
• Pan-African Congress delegates, 1921, unknown photographer. New York Public Library. Public Domain.

Chapter 11
• Cité Mondial concept, Paul Otlet and Hendrik Christian Anderson, 1924, Mundaneum Wallonia-Brussels Federation collection research archives and European Commission for Culture and Creativity. Public Domain.
• Paul, Mathilde & Henri outside the Palais Mondial, 1930, Mundaneum Wallonia-Brussels Federation collection research archives and European Commission for Culture and Creativity. Public Domain.
• Cité Mondial planners Le Corbusier and Paul Otlet, 1929, Geneva GNU Free Documentation. Public Domain.

Chapter 12
• Paul Otlet, Mundaneum 20th anniversary portrait, 1931, Mundaneum Wallonia-Brussels Federation collection research archives and European Commission for Culture and Creativity. Public Domain.
• Paul Otlet, alone in the Mundaneum. Mundaneum Wallonia-Brussels Federation collection research archives and European Commission for Culture and Creativity. Public Domain.
• Henri La Fontaine and Paul Otlet, Universal Peace Conference, 7 July 1931, Mundaneum Wallonia-Brussels Federation collection research archives and European Commission for Culture and Creativity. Public Domain.
• Collapse of German banking system, 13 July 1931, Bundesarchiv Bild 102-12023 Berlin. Public Domain.

Chapter 13
• Paul Otlet, 1934, Mundaneum Wallonia-Brussels Federation collection research archives and European Commission for Culture and Creativity. Public Domain.
• Henri La Fontaine, 1934, Fondation Henri La Fontaine, Federation Wallonie-Bruxelles, Francophones Bruxelles. Public Domain.

Chapter 14
• Document 8440, sketch design for the Internet, 1934, Paul Otlet. Mundaneum Wallonia-Brussels Federation collection research archives and European Commission for Culture and Creativity. Public Domain.
• Document 8441, sketch design for the Internet, 1934, Paul Otlet. Mundaneum Wallonia-Brussels Federation collection research archives and European Commission for Culture and Creativity. Public Domain.
• the note from Wilhelmina Coops to Paul Otlet, 1934. Mundaneum Wallonia-Brussels Federation collection research archives and European Commission for Culture and Creativity. Public Domain.

• Traité de Documentation title page, by Paul Otlet, 1934. Mundaneum Wallonia-Brussels Federation collection research archives and European Commission for Culture and Creativity. Public Domain.
• series of diagrams from Traité de Documentation, by Paul Otlet, 1934. Mundaneum Wallonia-Brussels Federation collection research archives and European Commission for Culture and Creativity. Public Domain.
• page 450, Traité de Documentation, by Paul Otlet, 1934. Mundaneum Wallonia-Brussels Federation collection research archives and European Commission for Culture and Creativity. Public Domain.

Chapter 15
• Paul Otlet at the former Palais Mondial archway, 1939, photographer unknown. Public Domain.
• Paul and Cato Otlet with the last of the Mundaneum team. Mundaneum Wallonia-Brussels Federation collection research archives and European Commission for Culture and Creativity. Public Domain.
• the abandoned Mundaneum, 1940, photographers unknown. Mundaneum Wallonia-Brussels Federation collection research archives and European Commission for Culture and Creativity. Public Domain.
• Henri La Fontaine mourns the Mundaneum, 1930. Photographer unknown, NobelPrize.org, Mundaneum via Wikimedia Commons. Public domain.
• surviving box files from the original Mundaneum, date unknown, with thanks to the Mundaneum museum, Mons. Mundaneum Wallonia-Brussels Federation collection research archives and European Commission for Culture and Creativity. Public Domain.

Chapter 16
• first day at the new school, 1907. Johann Heinrich Döll Verlag, Bremen. Public Domain.

- Kaiser Wilhelm II, in Death's-head Hussar uniform. W. Stanley Macbean Knight postcard. 1910. Public Domain.

Chapter 17
- Ludendorff and Hitler, leaders of the beer hall riot 1923. Bundesarchiv, Bild 102-00344A / Heinrich Hoffmann / CC-BY-SA. Public Domain.
- 20 billion Reichsmark note, 1923. Reichsbankdirektorium Berlin, Godot13, National Numismatic Collection, National Museum of American History. Public Domain.

Chapter 18
- Germania City concept, Adolf Hitler and Albert Speer, 1939, German Federal Archive Cooperation Project, Creative Commons Attribution. Public Domain.
- Germania planners Albert Speer and Adolf Hitler, 1943, photographed by Eva Braun, National Digital Archives, Poland and National Archives College Park. Public Domain.

Chapter 19
- Launch of the luxury liner SS Bremen 1929, Bundesarchiv Bild 102-11081. Public Domain.
- Friemaurer geschmiedet durch die Werkzeuge seiner Loge, 1754. Public Domain.

Chapter 20
- NSDAP membership card 159,203, reproduction, Kraus Papierwerke, Dornbiern. Mel Croucher private archive.
- Sturmableitung uniform doll, Germania International, anonymous family collection SA-41, 1945. Public Domain.

Chapter 21
- Student incitement poster. Ludwig Hohlwein, Munchen, 1933. Denazification archive. Public Domain.
- Students preparing for the rally, 6 May 1933. Photographer unknown. United States Holocaust Memorial Museum. Public Domain.

• Bookburners, Germany, 10 May 1933. Universal History Archive. Photographer unknown. Public Domain.

Chapter 22
• Chancellor Hitler and President Hindenburg, 1933. Ann Ronan Picture Library donation. Public Domain.
• Nazis take their seats in Parliament, 1932, SZ Photo. Public Domain.
• Helli and Phillip Bouhler, 1934, Peter D.O. photographic studio. Public Domain.

Chapter 23
• Form and Development of the Reich, by Hans Hagemeyer, book cover, Propylaen-Verlag, Berlin, 1940. Public Domain.
• Europe's Fate in the East, by Hans Hagemeyer, book cover, Ferdinand Hirt Verlag, Breslau, 1938. Public Domain.
• Mont Blanc silver swastika fountain pen, Eberswalde, 1941. Gallerie d'Histoire André Hüsken. Public Domain.
• 10 November 1938 Nuremburg, Kristalnacht looting of Jewish books, family archive of Elisheva Avital donated to Yad Vashem Holocaust Museum, Jerusalem. Public Domain.

Chapter 24
• Hans Hagemeyer, Head of Reich Office for the promotion of German Literature. Scherl, Süddeutsche Zeitung 1936. Public Domain.
• Audience listening to Hans Hagemeyer at the third session of the Reich Office for the Promotion of German Literature, Scherl, Süddeutsche Zeitung 1936. Public Domain.
• Entry to Parc Cinquantenaire, Brussels, 1930s, postcard, photographer unknown, Public Domain.

Chapter 25
• All Germany listens to the Führer on the People's Radio, poster 1936, Bundesarchiv Koblenz and United States Holocaust Memorial Museum, Washington. Public Domain.

• Public television Parlour, Berlin, 1935, Bundesarchiv Bild/Orbis-Photo. Public Domain.
• Der Stürmer weekly newspaper, street display, 1941, United States Holocaust Memorial Museum, Washington. Public Domain.

Chapter 26
• Hans Hagemeyer, Member of Parliament, Scherl, Süddeutsche Zeitung 1941. Public Domain.

Chapter 27
• approved German Christmas card, 1941, designer unknown, with permission from Elinor Florence family private collection, Canada.
• Yule tree bauble, 1941, manufacturer unknown, with permission from private collection of Hitler's Only Got One Bauble, Claus Dalsborg, Denmark.
• Julleuchter Yule Lantern, 1941, Nordic Museum, Stockholm, Public Domain.

Chapter 28
• Mother's Cross Award, designed by Franz Berberich, statutory legislation of the Deutsches Reich Law Gazette Part I, No. 224, 1938. Public Domain.
• Ausstellung "Frau und Mutter - Lebensquell des Volkes" Weltbild, Austrian National Library, Public Domain.
• Frau und Mutter, book cover, Hoheneichen Verlag München 1942, de-Nazification compulsory dissolution 1945. Public Domain.

Chapter 29
• Hans Hagemeyer, 2nd left, opening of Great German Exhibition, former site of the Mundaneum, Brussels. Scherl, Süddeutsche Zeitung 1942. Public Domain.

Chapter 30
• central Berlin after RAF air raids of December 1944. Mel Croucher, family private archive.
• Destruction of the German archives, 1944, United States Holocaust Memorial Museum, Washington. Public Domain.
• Alfred Rosenberg, 1944, United States Holocaust Memorial Museum, Washington. Public Domain.
• Hans Hagemeyer, 1944, Wikimedia Commons. https://creativecommons.org/publicdomain/mark/1.0/deed.en. Public Domain.

Chapter 31
• Paul Otlet 1868-1944, untended grave, by AK Kennedy, 26 October 2021. Creative Commons International licence, free media repository. Licence deed https://creativecommons.org/publicdomain/zero/1.0/

Chapter 32
• Hans Hagemeyer, acting in 'The Last Blitzkrieg' 1958. Private archive, Mel Croucher.
• Paul Otlet, with model of Cité Mondial. Wikimedia Commons. https://creativecommons.org/publicdomain/mark/1.0/deed.en. Public Domain.

Author's Afterword
• Paul Otlet and Jiddu Krishnamurti, 1926, Mondothèque Free documentation license. Public Domain.

UK copyright.
Photographic and pictorial images used in this publication that are over 70 years old and where the copyright owner has been dead for more than 70 years fall under the public domain fair use category in UK law, *Intellectual Property Office, Copyright Notices, updated 4 January 2021.*

EU copyright.
Photographic and pictorial images used in this publication that are over 70 years old and where the copyright owner has been dead for more than 70 years fall under the public domain fair use category in EU law, *Article 14 Directive on Copyright of the European Parliament Committee on Legal Affairs 12 September 2018*.

US copyright.
Photographic and pictorial images used in this publication and published in the United States before 1929 are in the public domain. Photographic and pictorial images published before 1964 whose copyright has not been renewed since then are in the public domain. Photographic and pictorial images used in this publication that are over 70 years old and where the copyright owner has been dead for more than 70 years fall under the public domain fair use category in US law, *Title 17 of the United States Code, 23 December 2022*.

Where copyright exists on any photographic or pictorial images used in this publication, ownership is acknowledged and accredited, and all necessary permissions and/or paid licences have been obtained and are included in the image credits above. Where paid licences are applicable, such licences extend to this publication *per se* as well as marketing and promotional usage, including: unlimited web usage across websites and social media, short form video on video sharing sites, digital and print marketing, web and social platforms, leaflets, brochures and emails, digital and print publications, newsletters, magazines and newspapers, print runs up to 100,000 copies.

other publications by MEL CROUCHER

Pimania the Final Solution (with Robin Evans)
1982, Automata

101 Uses of a Dead Cruise Missile (with Robin Evans),
1983, Scorpio Ltd / PCND

The Back Pages (with Robin Evans)
1983-1985, Sunshine Publications, weekly

Tamara Knight
1986, Newsfield Publications, monthly

Mercy Dash (with Robin Evans)
1986-1988, Dennis Publishing, monthly

Rebel of World Zero (with Robin Evans)
1987-1988, EMAP Publications, monthly

Without Prejudice
1987-1989, Stranger Than Fiction, monthly

Frozen Stiffs (with Robin Evans)
1987-1989, Stanger Than Fiction, monthly

Namesakes (with Jon Pertwee)
1988, Sphere Books, ISBN 780747400233

European Computer Trade Yearbook (as Editor)
1988-1995, ECTA, annually

Zygote, Last Words
1988-2020, Dennis Publishing, monthly

AMOS Professional
1989, Europress, ISBN 0951953214

Sam Coupé
1989, Miles Gordon Technology, ISBN 9781785388613

Easy AMOS
1992, Europress, ISBN 781872084527

e-media
2000, Institute of Practitioners in Advertising, ISBN 1841160555

Deus Ex Machina
2014, Acorn Books, 9781783336937

From Bedrooms to Billions (as himself)
2014, Gracious Films, ISBN 700461458784

Devil's Acre
2015, Acorn Books, ISBN 978-1837910731

Great Moments In Computing (with Robin Evans)
2017, Acorn Books, ISBN 9781785387579

Pibolar Disorder (with Robin Evans)
2017, Acorn Books, ISBN 9781785388330

Short Pants (with Robin Evans)
2017, Acorn Books, ISBN 9781785388309

Last Orders
2017, AG Books ISBN 1785386417

Memoirs of a Spectrum Addict (as himself)
2017-2020, RAM Films

Mel Croucher the Audiobook
2017, Oak Tree Press/Andrews UK, ASIN B074VHGZMD

Great Moments in Computing, the Complete Edition
2022, Acorn Books, ISBN 9781789829242

Additional details of Mel Croucher's work are available on Wikipedia: https://en.wikipedia.org/wiki/Mel_Croucher and on the official Mel Croucher website: www.melcroucher.net

For details of new and forthcoming books from Extremis Publishing, including our monthly podcast, please visit our official website at:

www.extremispublishing.com

or follow us on social media at:

www.facebook.com/extremispublishing

www.linkedin.com/company/extremis-publishing-ltd-/